OUR DAYS ARE NUMBERED

The Greatest Revelation of all Time

JD McKenzie

ORIGINAL WRITING

Pat,

a signed copy of the book —
to challenge you.
The findings are remarkable
enough to say aloud 'Eureka'.

JD McKenzie
2009

OUR DAYS ARE NUMBERED

The Greatest Revelation of all Time

JD McKenzie

First published 2002 ISBN 0-9543427-0-4
The moral right of the author has been asserted.

Revised Edition 2009
ISBN 978-1-906018-86-3

A CIP catalogue for this book is available from Trinity College, Dublin, Ireland.

Published by Original Writing Ltd., Dublin, 2009.
www.originalwriting.ie

Printed by Cahills, Dublin.

www.ourdaysnumbered.com

Dedicated to Natasha

Gomel

Цветок Готеля

Do passing scenes exist
Or just mere pictures
Forming in our mind?
Those green fields
Are not there
When I'm not there,
It is time that makes them real

Time is now
Where we wait,
While we stand still
The earth's still spinning
Through time, through time
Never to return
Still, standing still

The nightfall
Makes the pictures disappear
Fading green fields are no more
Darkness brings sleeping darkness
Where dreams awaken fears

Seasons blossoms fade
Age grows grey
Snow falls quietly
A white shade
and then we see
The land that used to be

In your country overnight
An unseen shadow did descend
Even time stood still
When winter came in spring

Twenty springs have since
passed
Words, like time, stand still
To say that we are here
By the strength of human will

In Gomel, when we meet there
Let us plant a tree and flowers
That they may grow in time
By the sun's sustaining hours

Наташе   Late Spring 2006

JD McKenzie

TABLE OF CONTENTS

PART II

CHAPTER 6

CHAPTER 7

TABLES

ACKNOWLEDGEMENTS

I would like to thank all those who helped me during the long years of research that finally led to this edition of 'Our Days Are Numbered.'

My special thanks to:

Tom Coogan	Jeanne Deegan	Aengus Fanning
Noel Stafford	Dave Halloran	Ciara Miller Farrell
John Walshe	Arlin Baldwin	Sharon Plunkett
Agnes Bryce	P.J. Cunnigham	Anne Marie Dolan
Paul Hyland	Eugene Healy	Susie Ciurana Coveney
Ray Kennedy	Robert Lomas	Gerry Fanning (deceased)

I would like to thank **Doctor Ari Belenkiy** for pointing out how the Bible was actually written and for referring me to certain biblical literature.

My appreciation also to **Doctor Kieran O'Mahony** for enlightening me on the unreliability of some numbers in the Bible.

I would also extend my thanks to the following authors whose books were of tremendous help to me:

'**Calendars In the Dead Sea Scrolls,**' James C. VanderKam;

'**Who Wrote the Bible,**' Richard Elliot Friedman;

'**How Jesus became Christian,**' Barrie Wilson;

'**Redeeming Time,**' Bruce Chilton;

'**The Jesus Mystery,**' Lena Einhorn.

Many thanks to Natallia Alampiyeva who helped me with the layout, design and illustrations of the book.

I would also like to thank my good friends in Belarus, Nina Linkevich and Aliaksei Zharkin.

On a personal level I would like to thank Maria, Julie, Roisin, Sinead, Aisling and Robert.

In memory of my mother Margaret and my father Michael and to acknowledge the inspiration they gave me.

PREFACE TO THE SECOND EDITION

Since the first edition of 'Our days are Numbered' was published in 2002 the research work continued and produced many wonderful discoveries. In hindsight, the first edition now looks like a freshly discovered archeological site that was just waiting for the trowels to remove the top soil. The digging has since taken place and from the depths of history the patterns have been identified that make the biblical numbers a jigsaw of time measurements Those patterns formed into a verification process that adhered to the principles of ancient Jewish mathematics where there must always be at least two witnesses to prove an outcome. Embedded in the intelligent design of the numerical embroidery was a unique encoding system that contained the blueprint of a sacred calendar. Interpreting the words of the Bible to suit the latest catastrophe and propel the end is nigh is commonplace and the Internet provides the instant mass media for such graffiti. Against that background it was never going to be easy to proclaim that something new had been deciphered from within the good book. That it was a discovery so momentous in numerical sophistication measuring out the history of the Israelites from their origins to demise thus seemed so far fetched as to be a soft target for ridicule. Despite those pitfalls someone has to put a foot forward and explore new territory. The Dead Sea scrolls were found by a Bedouin boy throwing a stone into a cave only to hear the sound of breaking jars. In contrast, the temple calendar was found in full public view much less than a stone's throw away. It was visibly displayed in the Bible before the curious gaze of millions, *but none could see.*

PROLOGUE

All epic stories are about discovery, trials triumphs, and revelations. Man always knew he would be tested. Whether it was to keep warm or feed his hungry children, the daily struggle to survive and the strength to prevail would always be a challenge. This business of existence, walking among the beasts of the earth, amid its hostile peoples was fraught with risk. The cost of seeing each sun rise and set had to be paid in blood and sweat. Man needed to know it was worth it. And so he looked to the heavens, where came the rains for him to sate his thirst and the sunlight to grow his crops. In the ceaseless motions of the planets he found comfort for they followed fixed patterns. He noted that if he organised himself in harmony with the sun he could sow his seeds and reap his harvests with hope. The bounty of the heavens was limitless, and this new gift of the orderly progression of events he came to call time; it would prove to be his most constant companion. Yet, even so, he at once knew that he would always be its servant. He would call it the Old Master.

The greatest epic story we know is the Bible. In it, Jesus comes to spread the good news that the game is most definitely worth the candle. Man will triumph over death, his great adversary, whom he is pitted against from birth. He will walk with God in the Heavens. But man was a sceptical creature. He needed to be. That tree trunk floating down river which might keep him warm for three days, might also be a crocodile which would eat him in three days! If he was going to rise up to the heights of God it was going to take some feat of engineering.

This Jesus had fed the hungry hordes and even becalmed the angry seas; or so we were told! But can you believe everything you hear? Not surprisingly the holy men and scribes were perplexed. They had walked and supped with Jesus. They knew him to be the real deal. It went beyond flamboyant trickery and showmanship. He lived the truth. In his calmness there was a divine confidence born out of conviction that went beyond faith. No mortal man, all too familiar with the unequal match between himself and the elements, could carry that off.

That Jesus rose and ascended to his Heavenly Father was all well and good. Many had seen enough to be convinced that it was so. But what of the other three billion doubting Thomases? Try selling the concept of eternity to parents who have lost their children to smallpox, or to the widows who have seen their husbands slain by marauding bandits. That kind of talk ended with being nailed upside down, with a crowd around you. And so they thought again. Had Jesus not said; "I am the way, the truth and the light. He who believes in me will live for ever....." If there was a practical way to demonstrate that forever really was within the grasp of slaves and Pharaohs alike, then perhaps.....that really would be a potent weapon for the armoury, one that would command respect and engage the attention of all.

And so the idea of a golden arrow in the quiver took flight in the mind's eye. One that might fly from the bow illuminating the path of God past the many mansions in the night skies, which mortal man could follow as it completed its arc to earth? Would that not be Divine? But then again even gold will lose its lustre and tarnish eventually. What is always with us and never ages? If the arrow was wrought from the very stuff of time and guided the way, what a construct that would be. Was it not true that from the very first time he stood in the noon day sun Jesus had cast a long shadow? Their quest was now to prove just how long that shadow would be. Using times arrow they would point the way.

The shadow of this mortal frame would be transformed into a sun dial to reach beyond the planets and establish a connection with the earth that would endure for all eternity. This would be the true path to the Lord Jesus, to God and through God. Thus a sacred time line would be created, one that would prove that Jesus was indeed the Messiah or Saviour. The very Heavens could be called upon to confirm his identity. Not only had a star shone in the East, but there would be myriad other irrefutable proofs to guide the way, the indices of which would be committed in the great book. This portal to the heavens would endure for all time because it was made of time itself. There would be many master-works made by the son of man that would give witness to God's inspiration. But long after even the Pyramids of Egypt returned to the sand and the roof of Michelangelo's Sistine Chapel caved in, the Temple Timeline, or Calendar of God would still be a wonder to overpower all others.

This is the story of how that wonder was re-awakened with this discovery. It is the greatest story never told about the Bible, and it reveals the most astonishing secret of all that has slumbered undisturbed for 2,000 years at its heart: The Bible is the story of time.

"Hath it not been told to you from the beginning? Have you not understood from the foundations of the earth? It is he that sitteth upon the circle of the earth, and the inhabitants thereof are like grasshoppers; that stretch out the heavens as a curtain, and spread them out as a tent to dwell in;.. Lift up your eyes on high, and behold you have created these things, that bringeth out their hosts by number; he calleth them all by names by the greatness of his might."
Isaiah 40 21 22 6

Raheen Church, Laois

INTRODUCTION

The year 2,000 or Y2K brought about the greatest global celebrations imaginable to hail the new millennium. That auspicious New Year's Day also led to dire expectations of an electronic doomsday where malfunctioning clocks would bring airplanes crashing and halt the universal wheels of commerce. As we now know, time moved on in its natural cycles oblivious of the artificial clock adorned with the numerals **1:1:2,000** of the Common Era. Almost 2,000 years previously the innovator of that bi-millennium magic rode into Jerusalem to be cheered by jubilant crowds who laid out a carpet of palms for their royal visitor. On that date, to the very day, Jesus fulfilled the greatest mission in patriarchal history where he travelled the last leg of an epic journey through a very sacred time period.

"In the beginning was the Word," or so the Good Book claims. But even before that there was something more profound – eternal, invisible without shape. There was time, that everlasting ether with no beginning and no end. Quite literally everything under the sun begins and ends with time. It is a universal premise. The findings of recent research show that the ancient Hebrews were obsessed with mastering time. Time was that abstract world of circular motions, which had confused the greatest civilizations throughout history. It was an invisible god that defied all the five natural senses. In its wake that invincible force of time presided over cycles of birth, growth and decay; the grim reaper of life and death. And, death was that final journey that nobody could avoid!

The biblical scribes had somehow acquired the knowledge to come to grips with time and even had formulas to circumvent or turn back the eternal clock of fate. In the earthly solar dimension, they openly declared their mastery of time where they stated in the Book of Exodus that the Israelites were in Egypt for 430 years to the very day. It seemed to be a boastful claim in the era where sundials were their digital clocks. But, the Egyptians did have a 365 day calendar, so the statement from Exodus could have some merit. It appeared that time was not just an earthly concept for the Bible outlined two episodes, which introduced the divine hand of the Lord. The first encounter was where the sun stood in the sky for a whole day and gave Joshua the upper hand in battle. In the second divine example, the prophet Isaiah turned back the clock of Ahaz by ten degrees thus allowing the dying King Hezekiah to live another fifteen years. Obviously, those two biblical encounters required a leap of faith to be taken seriously. But not so for the mathematics with that unusual clock of Ahaz for those ten degrees representing fifteen years held an inherent secret. It was from evidence such as the 430 years to the very day in Egypt and the arithmetic inherent in the clock of Ahaz that led to the discovery of a truly unique biblical calendar system.

To accept the enormity of this discovery it must be seen in the context of the two great scholarly fixations of the period: the study of the stars and the manipulation of numbers. It is essential to understand that the scribes had a unique mastery of numbers and that knowledge included simple formulae to define, manage and circumvent what they saw as the evils of orbital time. These findings will show that the ancient Hebrews had somehow acquired what was, in effect, a calendar of the gods, which gave them the awesome power to literally track time into infinity. That calendar had a number of striking characteristics including:

- A sacred year that was 777 days long. For reasons yet to be outlined that sacred period has been termed the Temple Year and the associated time structure will be called the Temple Calendar.

- A numbering system that was encoded in the numerals of seven burnt offerings.

- Seven time periods measured to the very day and stretching from Abraham, Isaac, Jacob, Solomon down to Jesus.

- The harmonising of the regular orbits of those three main luminaries, Jupiter, Saturn and Venus with lengthy periods of solar years.

- A validation process with seven checksums to demonstrate to future researchers that the numbers in the burnt offerings had retained their original values intact.

- Numbers, operational instructions and formulae that were archived in the Torah. Those numerical assets were disguised as the counting system inherent in the two censuses of the tribes of Israel. It is now known that those two banks of numbers were inserted by a priestly author called P when the Torah was re-edited between 500-700BCE. The largest part of that archive not surprisingly became known as the Book of Numbers. Checksums were also included with those numbers to prove that they had retained their original values intact.

- Worship centrally at the temple which was en-compassed within the walls of Jerusalem. Several of the prophets were anxious that those walls should be mea-sured with a plumb line. That measurement proved to be profound.

The ability to read and understand the numerical system ap-pears to have been lost in history. But that was also the fate of the hieroglyphics until a French explorer found the Rosetta stone with its Greek and demotic Egyptian translation.

In nature time moves in cycles bringing the elements of spring, summer autumn and winter each with their corresponding life patterns of birth, growth, maturity and decay. In contrast, calendar time is linear and it is the platform on which we outline our history. i.e. Time is measured with a calendar in units of days, weeks, months and years as a straight forward process rather than by the rhythms of nature. The concept of linear time first features in the Book of Daniel in the reference on 2,300 days. Whitrow referred to linear time as progressive time and made an interesting observation as follows:

"Before the rise of Christianity, with the exceptions of a few isolated writers like Seneca, only the Hebrews and the Zoroastrian Iranian appear to have thought of history as a progressive rather than cyclic…the key to the Old Testament.. is the Book of Daniel, where history was presented under the guise of prophecy, as a unified process conforming to a divine plan." Whitrow P16

That notion of linear time being presented in the guise of prophecy as a unified process conforming to a divine plan had supercharged the earlier findings of the research when the numbers and equations were unraveling. The statement demonstrated that the blueprint of the temple calendar about to be outlined was not just a numerical jigsaw but, was in fact, an integral part of the religious belief system.

The evidence suggests that the purpose of the divine calendar was to map out time in sacred years of 777 days. That factor was simple enough to diagnose even if it took over 2,000 to discover the unique temple calendar itself. It took painstaking cross referencing through the myriad of numbers in the Bible to determine if the perceived 777-day temple year formula behaved as a calendar. The findings reveal that such biblical periods as 150 days, 5 months, 42 months and many other time intervals fit into the calendar structure, like as if they were made to measure. Those specific periods mentioned are cited in the Books of Genesis and

Revelation and have been the subject of speculation from scholars and sleuths alike for thousands of years. But, it was only with the benefit of the 777-day temple year that those intervals fulfilled a calendar leap day purpose.

There are many intriguing stories in the Bible and therein stands the genesis of this unique episode of time. The historical layout of the good book would lead to the belief that the Messiah time line story began when three men from God visited the aged Abraham and predicted that his childless-90-year-old wife Sarah would conceive and bear a son. Time's unnatural forces were evident again for amazingly, Sarah overcame age and conceived. That event set in train a forecasted time frame, which was to be measured out with the temple 777-day year. The findings will show that the concept of a Messiah and saviour was actually cast back in time by the prophet Isaiah et al to that period with Abraham. It may seem to be an unbelievable statement to comprehend but these findings are supported by those two genealogies in Mathew's and Luke's Gospels. From those two genealogies, it has been possible to identify and recreate the inherent time frame which shows a period of 1,680 years from Abraham to Jesus. Running in parallel with those two genealogies was the most sacred time period in biblical perfection for it was 777 temple years long. (777 days by 777 times) The importance of the sacred time line suggests that priests and scribes throughout the generations were adhering to that religious imperative and that biblical history was superimposed on the associated time line.

Time was not easy to predict and the straight path of the solar related temple calendar was forever in conflict with the unreliability of orbital time. To circumvent that evil conflict, the Hebrew's made atonement and devised the formulas to overcome those transgressions. Those devised formulas dictated that the regular orbits of Jupiter, Saturn and Venus would always be in harmony with the true heavenly body of solar time. Thus, the historical portrayal of events was overwritten into a unique parallel time line that had divine projections. Many characters linked with both those genealogies would carry the torch through biblical history with religious fervour. The last in line was afforded the mantle of saviour of Israel. Thus, when Jesus entered Jerusalem, he had travelled the last leg of that epic time journey culminating in 777 temple years to the very last day. It was signaled so mysteriously as "the end of days."

Any encounter with the Bible involves traversing sacred ground and perhaps glancing off many cherished beliefs. But this endeavour is not about sacking the temple, though it will certainly annul some of the myths and practices that religious establishments have rested on for thousands of years. However, in their place the findings do unveil the format of a magnificent numerical sophistication in all its multi-layered ingeniousness. The revelation that some of the most beautiful lyrical parables of the Bible as well as some of its most disturbing texts, carried a watermark that can only be seen when held up to the light of mathematics may seem controversial at first. Yet, the results will show that the days were forecast by the prophets from the beginning with Abraham to the end of days with the Messiah. It was to become the most successful exercise of pre-planning in history.

There was a particular facet with regard to the findings in this research that needs to be specifically highlighted. The results and calculations throughout the research work conform to the principle of ancient Jewish mathematics. Jewish scholasticism operated on the principle of economy where there was no special virtue in elaborate explanations when a simple hypothesis would cover the essential facts. There was nothing superfluous in scripture and a general principle only needed one specific case to illustrate it as being profound. If two examples were illustrated it conveyed that a special case was evident and occurred in a limited set of situations. The Bible cites that there must be two witnesses to substantiate an accusation. In this light, to have three witnesses would result in a sound conviction. The arithmetical results in this research conform to this category of having two witnesses to authenticate the findings. But, there are some notable exceptions where three examples provide that critical stamp of definable proof. Note 1

PART I

Jerusalem

CHAPTER 1

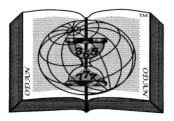

THE TEMPLE CALENDAR UNVEILED

The biblical scribes created the most successful encryption code in history. Unlike the ingenuity of modern security techniques with secret PINs and alpha-numeric codes, the Bible displayed its encrypted message openly before our very eyes. In fact, it was so obvious to see but yet so difficult to comprehend. It would appear the scribes were very much aware that the minds eye has an aversion to numbers. Most people are content to read the text but inadvertently skip over numbers. That was the key that possibly safeguarded the encryption code from the scholarly hackers through thousands of years. But, the biblical authors seemingly wanted to get caught for they left a trail of clues to taunt us. There most avid clues were with prompts of the number seven. Seven was the most sacred number of the ancient Hebrews and clusters of three sevens appeared many times in close proximity throughout the Bible. For instance, the walls of Jericho fell down when seven priests circled the city seven times for seven days and blew on seven trumpets while the Israelites gave a tremendous goal-scoring type shout. Seven was also evident with the mighty Samson and his seven locks of hair while he pushed the mill wheel round and round. Those two examples created an image of circular motions with sevens in each cycle.

That image developed into reality with the temple calendar and it has been possible to recreate the original structure through a simulation exercise with solar time. By measuring time in lots of 777 days the result revealed that there was a harmonious relationship with the solar year of 365 ¼ days. Note 2 At regular focal points the 777 day temple year crossed the path of the solar year to intersect it at almost the exact same anniversary day. It will be shown that the importance of having sacred festivals on the same anniversary date were religious imperatives to the ancient Hebrews. For the purpose of this research the exercise was simulated theoretically by counting out the days in lots of 777 and it resulted with those unexpected findings. It was discovered that after counting out 55 lots of 777 days the count returned to the same anniversary as the starting birth date after the period of 117 years. All that was required was to make a leap period adjustment of just 1 day 16 hours (in fractional terms 1 ⅔ days) to synchronise the time exactly with the solar year. The next anniversary day was when 102 lots of 777 days were counted out to stop at 217 years. It only required an additional 3 ½ leap days to reach the exact anniversary day. Thus, this system of counting out the days one by one to reach 777 days and then repeating the process to reach 55 and 102 temple years was the blueprint for a reliable long term solar calendar. Note 3 Just as with the image at the walls of Jericho, time went round and round in cycles of 777 days to measure out other long term periods to the same anniversary date, which were 334, 451, 568, 668, 902 and 1,002 years. That was a theoretical simulation exercise but could the results be substantiated? It was time to test the theory and search for evidence in the Bible that would support the numerical findings.

The results from the search through the Bible proved that the prominent numbers of the temple calendar had been inserted in seven burnt offerings. Note 4 Those burnt offerings were sacred ceremonies where sacrifices of animals were offered up to the

Lord and the congregation feasted on the meat. They were held on particular days such as with the Passover or First-fruits and would have been the equivalent of the sacred Christian festivals of Easter and Christmas. Two of those burnt offerings were made during the reign of King Hezekiah who was in power around 720 BCE. The first of those offerings entailed seven bullocks, seven rams and seven lambs being sacrificed. Isaiah was a contemporary of Hezekiah and he stated that when dealing with the Egyptians the following should apply:

"Now go, write it before them in a table, and note it in a book, that it may be for the time to come for ever and ever." Isaiah 30:7:8.

The instruction clearly distinguishes between writing in a table and making a note in a book and aptly, it specifically related to eternity in time. That cluster of three sevens took on a more meaningful look when presented in tabular form as follows:

Bullocks	Rams	Lambs
7	7	7

It seemed plausible that the numbers in that presentation were intended to mean the actual number of 777. In that regard, the lambs would represent units, the rams tens and the bullocks hundreds.

Travelling back through the Bible brought the research to Chapter 29 of the Book of Numbers where burnt offering sacrifices were also made. The main offerings comprised of one bullock, one ram and seven lambs. Applying a tabular presentation to those numbers revealed the following:

Bullocks	Rams	Lambs
1	1	7

What was materialising was striking for in that tabular format the number 117 was evident. From the results of the simulation exercise so far it appeared that the burnt offerings with the 7 bullocks, 7 rams and 7 lambs was the number 777 to represent days. Therefore, the offering with 1 bullock, 1 ram and 7 lams would be 117 as years. If this theory held true the principle of a unique solar calendar certainly seemed to be emerging.

The attention switched to the burnt offering in Chapter 28 of the Book of Numbers. There were three similar numerical offerings one of which was to be made on the feast of the Passover. The offerings consisted of two bullocks, one ram and seven lambs. From that preview it was already evident that the great secret of the Bible was unravelling for in the tabular presentation the number was as follows:

Bullocks	Rams	Lambs
2	1	7

Yes, the number 217 was clearly evident. Therefore, all the three numbers of 777, 117 and 217 which were the focal point of the search had been found in the most sacred ceremonial offerings of the ancient Hebrews. That simulation of measuring time with the 777 day temple year had thus proved to be the key that unlocked the greatest encryption code ever devised in human thought.

Numbers can play tricks with the mind so it was necessary to ground the results by establishing if there were some extra related figures to reinforce those initial findings. Such related figures would be the leap days necessary to harmonise multiples of the 777 day temple year with 117 and 217 years to the very day. The leap days with the 117 year period was 1 ⅔ days while the leap day for the 217 year period was 3 ½ days. Therefore, the presence of fractions was the focus of attention and peculiarly, there were fractions of flour and oil to be mingled with the sacrifices in both Chapters 28 and 29 of the Book of Numbers. The total of those fractions added up to 3 ½ in Chapter 28, which was where the 217 had been deciphered and they compared exactly to the 3 ½ leap days in 217 years. Likewise, the total of the fractions in chapter 29 where the 117 was deciphered were 1.6 and that result compared to 1.66 leap days in 117 years. Thus, the leap days of the two periods of 117 and 217 years matched up very favourably with the fractions in each respective chapter where the numbers had been deciphered. There were two matching results, which was in keeping with the bibles own truth test where there should be two witnesses to corroborate a fact.

The outcome so far had demonstrated that at least some of the numbers in the Bible served a disguised purpose and were not just historical accounts of animals or weights and measures. It was therefore enlightening to fine out that a comprehensive editing of the Torah took place and large inserts of a priestly document were inserted in the book around 500BCE. Note 5 The most noticeable aspect about those insertions was that they consisted of large hosts of numbers together with many mathematical instructions. There had to be a real purpose for the biblical re-editors inserting those numbers and their values must have been of tremendous importance. The research had proven successful so far because those numbers of animals had been utilised as neutral figures. Therefore, for the remainder of this exercise all biblical numbers will be treated as neutral figures and examined for time related properties. The utilisation of those inserted numbers from the Torah to construct a unique calendar can now begin.

THE YEARS OF TEMPLE TIME

The theoretical simulation of measuring time with the 777 day temple year had resulted with the following periods where the solar year was in harmony with the temple year:

117 – 217 – 334 – 451 – 568 – 668 - 685 – 785 – 902 - 1002 years

All those periods had less than 4 leap days. The scribes had included those possible combinations where they inserted three lots of 217 and 117 as part of the burnt offerings in Chapters 28 and 29 of the Book of Numbers. It allowed for the formation of those longer terms of years E.g. 217 + 117 = 334 and 217 + 117 + 117 = 451 + 117 = 568 etc. While it was a novel system to measure time with great accuracy the periods involved were rather difficult to comprehend. In contrast our linear method of measuring long periods of time is in the metric numbers of 100, 200, 300 to 1,000, 2,000, 3000 years etc. and it is far simpler to administer. The notion of linear time seemingly did not figure with ancient calendars and indeed the dating method for measuring back in time before Christ BC was only devised in recent centuries. But the concept of linear time did feature in the Book of Daniel relative to the statement on 2,300 days as outlined in the earlier reference by Whitrow. That made it all the more interesting to establish if the Hebrews had employed the concept of using linear periods of 100 years in their unique calendar? Note 6

There were seven burnt offerings relative to this biblical calendar and fittingly, one of them was made by Solomon on being crowned king. He made the offering on the morning after his father David died and it consisted of one thousand bullocks, one thousand rams and one thousand lambs The tabular numerical format was as follows:

Bullocks	Rams	Lambs
1000	1000	1000

Naturally the presentation could not form into a number with units, tens and hundreds. Rather its numerical contents were three sets of 1,000. But were those three numbers intended as three periods of 1,000 years? If so then the matching leap days for one period of 1,000 years when measured by the temple yearly calendar would be 52 days to be added on. There was no evidence of 52 leap days accompanying those burnt offerings.

The next burnt offerings to be considered were those made by King Hezekiah and the first such offering was already outlined with its inherent value of 777. But the king made a second burnt offering which consisted of 70 bullocks, 100   rams and 200 lambs. Those numbers were then presented in tabular format as follows:

Bullocks	Rams	Lambs
70	100	200

Those numbers could not form one single meaningful number but they could represent the three periods of 70, 100 and 200 years. If they were intended as periods of years then the 70 years would later prove to be a fundamental element of the calendar albeit as another constituent element. The next burnt offering was made by Ezra and it consisted of 100 bullocks, 200 rams and 400 lambs, which are presented in tabular format as follows:

Bullocks	Rams	Lambs
100	200	400

Just like the two previous burnt offerings, the hunch was that those three numbers represented the three periods of 100, 200 and 400 years. If that were the case and leaving aside the 70 years in the previous burnt offering for the moment, the following periods were evident:

$$100 + 200 + 100 + 200 + 400 = 1,000 \text{ years}$$

Those numbers as time periods were like stepping stones to reach 1,000 years. If the theory of those numbers representing years held true then 1,000 years was the principal number of linear time and the quest would thus be to find 52 to represent leap days and 1,000 relative to years.

In the search for that combination of numbers it was noticed that the last five burnt offerings had been made centrally in Jerusalem. The focus of the search was a measurement and in that regard Barclay pointed out that the picture of measuring was common in the visions of the seers and the prophets throughout the Bible. Note 7 The one main theme of those references was about using a plumb line to measure the walls of Jerusalem. Just like linear time, a plumb line measures in a straight line.

The walls of Jerusalem were rebuilt by Nehemiah and there was a whole episode about the organisation to fulfil that task. It stated that the wall of Jerusalem was 1,000 cubits long and:

"The wall was finished in the twenty and fifth day of the month Elul, in fifty and two days." Nehemiah 6:15

The number was 1,000, albeit in cubits and the wall of Jerusalem took 52 days to complete. The search was for the number 1,000 to represent years with an associated number of 52 to represent the extra leap days. The burnt offerings were made centrally at the temple encircled by the city walls of Jerusalem that were 1,000 cubits long. The evidence was both substantial and

The Walls of Jerusalem

consistent to corroborate the verdict that 1,000, with its associated 52 days was intended by the scribes. Thus, the new name of Temple Calendar seemed appropriate.

There was still the last burnt offering to be examined and it was also made by Ezra. The numerical contents of that offering appeared to belong to the orbital time of the Zodiac. It consisted of twelve bullocks, ninety six rams and seventy seven lambs, which had the following tabular presentation:

Bullocks	Rams	Lambs
12	96	77

In that format the numbers could be considered to represent 129,677 years. Five cycles of the Zodiac equalled 129,600 years and it would appear from other results presently under research that that period was the target. Naturally, the end two digits with 77 lambs were obviously inserted because there could not be an offering of zero, zero lambs. The reference to the Zodiac may appear out of character with biblical script but nothing could be further from the case. In that regard, Whitrow outlined the beliefs of the heretical form of Zoroastrianism on 'the Time of the Long Dominion' as follows:

"A distinction was made between Zurvan akarna (infinite time) and 'Time of the Long Dominion' (finite time), the later lasting 12,000 years (the number twelve being associated with the 12 signs of the Zodiac) is the period of struggle between good and evil. In fact the whole raison d'etre of finite time appears to have been to bring about that conflict of good and evil which leads to the ultimate triumph of the good." Whitrow P16

Seemingly, it was well known that the ancients were involved in measuring the finite time period of 12,000 years and the author also referred to the figure twelve being associated with the twelve signs of the Zodiac. Finite time was the same as linear time, which was measured in a straight line direction in periods of 100, 1000, 10,000 years etc. In contrast the orbital time of the Zodiac was in infinite time. The statement from Whitrow showed that the whole *raison d'etre* of finite time was to bring about the conflict of good and evil which would lead to the ultimate triumph of the good. The central theme of biblical religion was encapsulated in that profound statement, the conflict between good and evil. The research had again ventured into the heart of religious belief where the measurement of time was not just a mere numerical exercise. It was an imperative core element of that particular belief system, a battle between good and evil, finite and infinite; the struggle with the invisible ether of time. The temple year of 777 days would prove to be the yardstick to measure those elusive times.

The measurement of temple time periods so far all related to solar calendar years. That situation left a vacancy in its train for it was essential to count out the days so as to measure out each solar year. There were numerous references in the Bible to events happening on particular days of the month but no actual calendar of days was set out that would have measured time. The Book of Jubilees did have a calendar system, which dated the events down from Adam but it was inculcated in the narrative while the book of Enoch adhered to a 364 day solar year. To reconstruct the temple calendar in its finer working detail it was essential to study the days of that peculiar almanac. There was a need to know the potential accuracy of the temple calendar and whether it was used to also measure out other high visibility orbits such as the regular periods of the planets. However, the absence of the days was not the only issue to address for the actual numbers in those burnt offerings also had to be evaluated. For instance, just how reliable were those numbers? After all, they were inserted in the Torah or included in the other biblical books well over two thousand years ago.

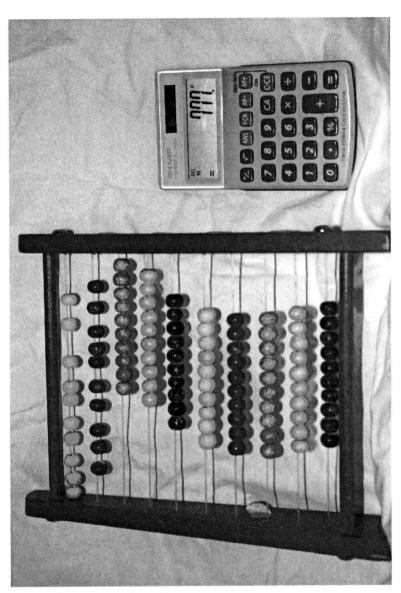

From Abacus to Calculator

CHAPTER 2

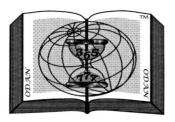

INFALLIBLE NUMBERS

D uring this research a biblical lecturer advised that the numbers in the Bible may not have retained their original values. For instance, some of the biblical numbers in the Ages of Adam have different values than the Greek Septuagint version. An example of this was where the final age of Lamech was 777 years in the bible as compared to 770 years in the Septuagint. Seemingly, the Bible was not so perfect after all. The patterns of two by two complimentary findings had bequeathed a degree of authenticity to the numbers in the burnt offerings. But, it was still desirable to establish if all of those numbers had retained their original values. Biblical scholars had debated the reliability of the numbers for generations so there was little prospect of finding evidence of the true value in ancient sources. There was however, the mathematical route to explore for in that medium the use of checksums could have been employed. Note 8

The numerical information from the Bible was being transmitted over thousands of years so the checksum total(s) would have to be in a format that was recognisable to every generation. In effect, a constant value would be vital for it to be recognisable over such lengthy periods. It will be shown later that the Hebrews had utilised the orbits of the three planets of Saturn, Jupiter and

Venus for time measurement. Therefore, it appeared reasonable to explore if the constant of orbital time would possibly be the checksum values. It was therefore necessary to list all the numbers of the seven burnt offerings and total them up as follows:

Bullocks	Rams	Lambs	
2	1	7	Numbers Ch. 28
2	1	7	Numbers Ch. 28
2	1	7	Numbers Ch. 28
1	1	7	Numbers Ch. 29
1	1	7	Numbers Ch. 29
1	1	7	Numbers Ch. 29
1,000	1,000	1,000	Chronicles1 29:21
7	7	7	Chronicles2 29:21
70	100	200	Chronicles2 29 32
100	200	400	Ezra 6:17
12	96	77	Ezra 8:35
Total: **1,198**	**1,409**	**1,726**	

Those totals were checked against the constants of orbital time and the following results as days were evident:

1. 1,409 as days proved to be 16 orbits of Mercury to within one leap day.

2. a. 1,198 + 1,726 = 2,924, which as days was 8 solar years to within two leap days.

    b. And 2,924 as days was also 99 lunar orbits.

    c. But 2,924 as days was also 13 orbits of Venus to less than three leap days.

It transpired that this eight year period was indeed very special for it was known as 'octaeteris' and knowledge of its uniqueness dated back to 500 BC. It was of great importance because it was very close to 99 lunar cycles of 29.53 days. Note 9 The eight solar years and the corresponding 13 orbits of Venus are referred to Earth and Venus being in resonance with each other. Note 10

3.   The period of 2,924 days was also 5 cycles of a special extra orbit of Venus which is known as the Synodic period. The leap day period was just 2 days to synchronise exactly with 8 solar years.

4.   The complete totals were 1,198 + 1,409 + 1,726 = 4,333. That result of 4,333 was the same numerical equivalent as one orbit of Jupiter to the exact whole day.

5.   Standing as the second witness to the orbit of Ju piter was where the number 1,198 when applied as years proved to be 101 orbits of that planet. There was an error of 31 leap days more than 1,198 solar years, which was just 7 hours 21 min utes for each of Jupiter's 11 years 314 day orbit.

It was an incredible result to comprehend and unlike the pattern of two by two witnesses that were so evident throughout the research findings, there were seven proofs. All that was expected was possibly one checksum to give a tacit authentication to those values in the burnt offerings. In that regard, the equivalent of one orbit of Jupiter at 4,333 would have seemed sufficient to fit that purpose, for that particular numerical value alone would be a remarkable encounter. But finding also the eight year period with the octaeteris relative to the solar and lunar harmony together with the 13 orbits of Venus in resonance was truly a profound discovery. Included in that 8 year period were 5 cycles of the Synodic period of Venus. There were also sixteen orbits of mercury thus making the checksums as credible as the word of God. Finally, the number 1,198 as years proved to be 101 orbits of Jupiter thus making the total of all the checksums that biblical sacred number of seven. Those checksums had also provided another profound function. They had validated that it was correct to utilise the decoded numbers of the burnt offerings with the units, tens and hundreds as 777, 117 and 217. Because of its strategic importance it was reasonable to suggest that the biblical age of Lamech as 777 years was the correct value whereas the Greek Septuagint age of 770 years was the wrong figure. Therefore, the framework of the temple calendar was not only clearly recognisable, but the numbers had a royal stamp of authentication with those seven checksums.

These finding so far were just the opening salver in identifying the framework of a biblical time line. However, missing from that framework was the absence of a calendar structure involving days, weeks and months. The Bible frequently referred to those periods of days and months but how they equated to this temple calendar was unknown. There are only three natural time periods and those are the solar day, lunar month and the solar year. The periods of a week or a calendar month are devised to structure our time so that we can function within an orderly framework. But the most basic unit of natural time was the solar day and all the other periods were multiples of it. How could the scribes have utilised the temple calendar with it lengthy periods in years without its micro component particles of days? Those yearly periods were secretly encrypted in the numbers of the burnt offerings. It was therefore conceivable that the days were also disguised in some major display of numbers.

The language of the Hieroglyphs written in Stone

CHAPTER 3

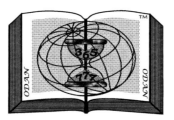

THE END OF DAYS TO THE MESSIAH

The burnt offerings with their distinctive numerical format began during the period of the Exodus out of Egypt. Therefore, the spotlight was on Moses when searching for a large scale bank of numbers that could be disguised as days. It outlined in the book of Jubilees that in the third month of the Exodus Moses was on Mount Sinai for forty days and forty nights and that God taught him:

"The earlier and later history of the division of all the days of the law and of the testimony" Jubilees CH. 1

Moses was told by God to write the information in a book. That statement was rather revealing to anyone looking for evidence of days. The earlier and later history of all the days, when taken literally, suggested the days were formed into divisions or arranged in some particular order. But there were also two arrangements: one being an earlier version while the other was more recent.

That earlier version would appear to have its origin with regard to watchers. There were many references to "The Watchers" in the Bible and in those terms, they could have been men on sentry look out, watching for hostile marauding bands. But seemingly, there was a very distinct duty for the watchers relative to observing the heavens. In the Book of Jubilees it refers to Kainam finding writing which former generations had carved on a rock. The writing contained:

"The teaching of the Watchers in accordance with which they used to observe the omens of the sun and moon and stars in all the signs of heaven" Jubilees Ch 8:3

The role of the watchers was very explicit for that statement shows them to be early astronomers. The writing on the rock was discovered long before Moses because Kainam was the great grandson of Adam. Therefore, the writing from the watchers was a good contender to be the earlier history of the divisions of the days. However, the focus of attention right now was for the later source of the division of the days relative to the events on Mount Sinai.

The divisions of the days would have required an exercise in the Torah involving a comprehensive numbering system to record time. There was no such evidence of counting the days but instead there was a massive exercise with Moses conducting two censuses of the tribes. The first such census occurred after the Israelites had travelled a year and a month through the wilderness. Each of the men of twenty years and upwards were counted by name and each man was numbered. Noticeably, the men were arranged in divisions. The numbers counted up to a total of 603,550 men in the first census and 601,730 in a second census that was held at the end of forty years in the wilderness. The size of those numbers being a population of men was rather hard to accept. It was also very peculiar to find out from biblical sources that those large banks of numbers in the two censuses were inserted in the Torah by that priestly author now called P at least 500 years after Moses. That certainly made those numbers extremely important, but why were they not recorded at the alleged time of the censuses? However, if those numbers were in fact the divisions of the days for measuring time, then the numerical insertions would have served a more profound purpose. It was necessary to take a more critical look at the numbers in those two censuses and also examine them in the context in which they were written.

It was more than obvious that the whole serial of the Exodus was dramatised and the size of the population given was clearly exaggerated. The total of the men of twenty years and upwards for the twelve tribes was listed as 603,550 in number while the Levites were counted separately and totalled 22,000. Allowing for the women, children, grandparents and grandchildren and others as stated in the Bible, the whole contingent would be in the region of two million people. That population was the size of a major modern city. Indeed, the city of New Orleans had a population of 1.4 million when hurricane Katrina struck. Contrast the plight of the inhabitants of New Orleans with the experience of the Israelites. The land of Egypt where they were enslaved had just suffered ten plagues that destroyed the water, animals and crops. There was also the image of a belligerent untrustworthy Pharaoh who continually ordered draconian treatment on the desperate Hebrew slaves. Then suddenly, after the slaughter of all the first born sons of the Egyptians by a vengeful god, the Israelites were freed by the grieving Pharaoh. The Bible tells us that the Israelites got out fast but yet they plundered the Egyptians but not of gold or material wealth. In contrast to the Exodus the mighty USA with all its vast resources was unable to cope with a partial evacuation of New Orleans.

The mystery continued for the obvious route for those two million Israelites to take was the straight bee line path through the desert into the promised land of milk and honey. Instead, they went in a semi-circle through the barren wilderness that took forty years to travel. There was no water in that rocky arid land to whet the thirst of those two million people and their vast herds and flocks. It would have needed a deluge to satisfy the thirst of that famished population. In that dire hour of need, Moses was portrayed like a conjurer when he struck a rock with his rod and miraculously produced a spout of water. The feat in all its glory would have delivered no more water than a village pump. Whether there was a stampede or not it does not say but the staff of Moses had in fact sufficed as a divining rod to find the source of water.

The focus was on the tribes of Israel so it was necessary to look back in time several hundred years before Moses to the founding father of those tribes, Jacob. There were twelve sons born to Jacob by his two wives, the sisters Leah and Rachel and their hand maids Zilpah and Bilah. Jacob had spent twenty years in Syria with his uncle Laban and was returning to his homeland with his family and vast herds and flocks. Something very unusual happened to him on that journey out of Syria that would alter the course and theme of biblical history. He had a visionary experience where he met the Lord and they had a wrestling match which went on all night. At dawn, Jacob was renamed and called Israel by the Lord.

It was to be a truly momentous event in the Bible for thereafter, Jacob and Israel were like two split personalities with regard to the biblical time line. In one account, Jacob was only one of seven generations from Abraham down to Moses. In the other account, there was 430 years between Jacob and his descendants who came out of Egypt, the Israelites. Two courses of history, two different stories and the later had all the hallmarks of 'make believe.' That encounter with the Lord brought into existence the Israelites. They would become that vast horde of two million slaves that had multiplied in Egypt. It was a huge population especially seeing that Jacob's family totalled seventy people when he went to live in Egypt 430 years earlier. The Book of Genesis was colourfully rich in biblical history and gave a detailed account of the adventures of Jacob. But then, there was a total silence for 430 years of history until the Exodus. Thereafter, history becomes alive again with a chronological outline of leaders and their exploits. Just what happened in those 430 years is unknown except the Israelites multiplied from just 70 people into a population of about two million people. But, on a closer scrutiny of the numbers of men in the first census a discovery came to light that would prove those figures to be a vast archive of time in days.

During the research work the presence of a luminary had been observed in the first count of the Tribes of Israel. That observation was where the numbers of the tribe of Benjamin in the 1st count beamed like a full moon. The total of those numbers were 35,400, which as days was one hundred lunar years. From that tell-tale sign it was decided to look back to see if there was anything of note in Benjamin's pedigree. Interestingly enough, there was a very odd incident that happened just before he was conceived. His mother Rachel had stolen her fathers images when her husband, Jacob was fleeing with his family and flocks out of Syria. Her father caught up with them and went searching the tents for those images. However, Rachel declared she had her period and so could not move from where she was sitting, which was on a camel's harness where the images were hidden. The specific mention of Rachel and her menstrual cycle suggested a linkage to the lunar cycle, which is somewhat similar in length, and both periods are ever so regular. The lunar year was a false god in time, it being only 354 days long, and the references to false images gave credence to that fact. Apparently, that was Rachel's last period for she conceived and died in childbirth while giving birth to her son Benjamin in a place called Bethlehem. And the numbers of the tribe of Benjamin in the first census proved to be one hundred lunar years.

From that observation with the tribe of Benjamin, the layers of camouflage disguised as two censuses soon came tumbling down. There was now a real purpose for those numbers having been inserted in the Torah and indeed, the quill of Isaiah was very evident. It could be said that he plotted that scene with the census for he referred to such a stage production profile when he wrote as follows:

"hath it not been told you from the beginning? Have ye not understood from the foundations of the earth? .. It is he that sitteth upon the circle of the earth, and the inhabitants thereof are like grasshoppers; that stretcheth out the heavens as a curtain, and spread them out as a tent to dwell in: ... Lift up your eyes on high, and behold you had created these things, that bringeth out their hosts by number; he calleth them all by names by the greatness of his might."
Isaiah 40 21 22 26

He sitteth upon the circle of the earth, bringeth out their hosts by number, he calleth them all by name. In the census of the twelve tribes of Israel each man was also called by name and numbered. The image suggested that those 603,550 men, in reality, were the hosts stretching out the heavens like a curtain? They were arranged in divisions, which is outlined in Chapter 2 of the Book of Numbers and noticeably, Moses had been dictated the divisions of the days on Mount Sinai. It was as if each man was assigned a day to carry like a bead on a huge abacus. In terms of manpower planning, the holy ones were counted out and the semi-circle in the wilderness was compassed to a phenomenal virtual period of 603,550 man-days. In that regard, Isaiah captured the steps in time almost like the droplets of a water clock with his colourful outline of grasshoppers jumping in equal steps to a natural rhythm.

That portrayal by Isaiah of the inhabitants being like grasshoppers was like a projection back in history, for when Moses sent out twelve men to spy out the Promised Land they referred to themselves in the eyes of the inhabitants as follows:

"And we were in our own sight as grasshoppers" Numbers 13:33

To the inhabitants they were like grasshoppers while spying out the Promised Land while Isaiah's statement had inhabitants like grasshoppers stretching out the heavens. The linkages of the words were quite stark but what of the numbers?

Those two censuses of the tribes must rate as the oddest but most intricate exercise in manpower planning and it came with an instruction manual. There were two censuses held, one after the first year in the desert and the other at the end of forty years. It was also noticed that the total of the 1st census at 603,550, as days, was just six months short of 777 temple years i.e. 777 days by 777 times. And Jesus was born six months after John. At this stage it was a long shot to co-relate the six months with John and Jesus, but yet it was a factor that will be evident at the end of this lengthy time period. The instructions were given by Moses that the two censuses were to be added together so as to apportion and settle distribution issues between the tribes. Note 11 It was also deducted that the total of the two censuses were then to be halved relative to a continual reference to the half tribe of Manasseh. Note 12

Those computations with the two censuses were carried out and entered into a table. It was necessary to include such relevant information as the order in which the sons of Israel were born together with their four respective mothers. The tribe of Levi was excluded from the twelve tribes and counted separately. Joseph was also excluded and he and Levi were replaced by Joseph's two sons, Manasseh and Ephraim. There were some switches in the order of place with the names of the tribes in the various listings.

The details are outlined in Table 1. Included with the table is an associated list of findings that emerged from a detailed analysis of the censuses. The first result from that analysed was as follows:

$$603,550 + 601,730 = 1,205,280 \div 2 = 602,640$$

The puzzle began unfolding for the result of 602,640, when interpreted as days, were the equivalent of 1,650 years. It was short of that period by nine leap days. Initially, the nine days error was not a problem for the Julian calendar accumulated an error of ten days before being corrected by Pope Gregory. Ironically, the lengthy period in time from Julius Caesar to Pope Gregory was also in the region of 1,650 years.

The research had reached a milestone, for there beyond direct view in half the totals of the 1st and 2nd census lay a secret vault of time. Those findings were so profound that this inner set of time measurements was named the Messiah time-frame. Even that nine day shortfall in the total of those man-days would prove to be deliberate for it served a major function.

A preview of the censuses and an analysis of the numbers in that table revealed the following:

- The 1st census was given in Chapter 1 and the 2nd census in Chapter 26 of the Book of Numbers. Both the censuses were added together and the total halved in accordance with instructions given in the Book of Numbers Ch.26:2:4:53:55:56 Ch 32:33

- Because ten of the numbers in the Messiah time-frame ended with a zero it could be expected that there would be a margin of error of ± 5 in any subsequent mathematical results. But surprisingly, most of the results were much more accurate.

Table 1: The two Census of the Tribes of Israel and the inner Messiah Time-frame

Names As Born	Mothers of sons	Names in 1st Count	1st Count		Names in 2nd Count	2nd Count	1st + 2nd Count	Messiah Time-frame
Reuben	Leah	Reuben	46,500		Reuben	43,730	90,230	45,115
Simeon	Leah	Simeon	59,300		Simeon	22,200	81,500	40,750
Levi	Leah	Gad	45,650		Gad	40,500	86,150	43,075
Judah	Leah	Judah	74,600		Judah	76,500	151,100	75,550
Dan	Bilah	Issachar	54,400		Issachar	64,300	118,700	59,350
Naphtali	Bilah	Zebulun	57,400		Zebulun	60,500	117,900	58,950
Gad	Zilpah	Ephraim	40,500	X	Manasseh	52,700	84,900	42,450
Asher	Zilpah	Mannaseh	32,200		Ephraim	32,500	73,000	36,500
Issachar	Leah	Benjamin	35,400		Benjamin	45,600	81,000	40,500
Zebulun	Leah	Dan	62,700		Dan	64,400	127,100	63,550
Joseph	Rachel	Asher	41,500		Asher	53,400	94,900	47,450
Benjamin	Rachel	Naphtali	53,400		Naphtali	45,400	98,800	49,400

- In the first census the totals of Leah's sons added up to 292,200, which as days was 800 years to within six leap days. That number of 292,200 was recognisable for it was also, in days, the length of one hundred 'octaeteris,' a period which was encountered earlier in the check-sums of the burnt offerings. The exact length of the solar year at 365.242 days is used in all the calculations in this research. But what length of year did our ancient friends utilise in their measurements? Applying our calendar year of 365.25 days would see the totals of Leah's five tribes at 800 years to the exact day.

- The totals of Leah's sons in the first census plus the numbers of Gad, which were the first six names all in sequence, added up to 337,850. That number 337,850 as days was 925 years to the very day.

- In the 2nd census the totals of Rachel's group of Ephraim, Manasseh and Benjamin together with Gad totalled 171,300, which was 469 years with only one leap day.

- The numbers of the first five tribes in sequence with the 2nd count and the numbers of Rachel's mini-group added up as follows:

$$43,730 + 22,200 + 40,500 + 76,500 +$$
$$64,300 + 52,700 + 32,500 + 45,600 \quad = 378,030$$

That total of 378,030 proved to be 1,035 years with just 4 leap days.

The Circle in the Sky

It was relatively easy to produce three of those results with their equivalent periods in years. They formed from Leah's group, the first five tribes in sequence plus Rachel's group in the 2nd count, and the first six tribes in sequence in the 1st count. The other result with Rachel's group plus Gad was not difficult to observe. It was therefore possible that there were other combinations of those numbers in the censuses that equated to time periods. Identifying those combinations was unlikely to be as easy as the initial findings above so evidence was sought to see if the scribes had left clues to help us create such formations. The main clues had been with the tribe of Benjamin with 35,400, which equated to 100 lunar years. That clue is again listed and it led to many more such clues as follows:

- The quote in the Gospels referencing Jeremiah relative to Rachel weeping for her children and of course, she died in childbirth giving birth to Benjamin in Bethlehem. Jesus was also born in Bethlehem and there was another reference stating his birth was at the time of a census. There was also a reference to a star of Bethlehem. The obvious clues were Bethlehem, a census and a star. Those clues pin-pointed the 1st census of the Tribes where the numbers of Benjamin, who was born in Bethlehem, were 35,400, which as days was 100 lunar years.

- When Jesus was being circumcised an elderly man called Simeon paid homage to him as did a woman called Anna who was from the tribe of Asher. Simeon and Asher together and their names formed two of the tribes so their numbers in both the 1st and 2nd census were examined and the following was evident:

-1st Census: Simeon at 59,300 + Asher at 41,500 = 100,800. As days that proved to be 276 years with just 7 leap days

-2nd Census: Simeon at 22,200 + Asher at 53,400 = 75,600. As days that proved to be 207 years with just 5 ½ leap days

- Because the clue came from the circumcision of Jesus on the 8th day, that period was added onto both the 276 and 207 years (almost) and the two results were profound. One derived from the solar year of 365.246 days (to the nearest 6 minutes) while the other derived from the exact sidereal year of 365.256 days. To get one such profound result would be unusual but to get the solar and sidereal years together in the same format was the Gospel truth.

Note. The solar year is measured by reference to a point on earth while sidereal year is measured by its alignment to a fixed star.

• In the first census the numbers of Gad, Ephraim, and Manasseh at 45,650 + 40,500 + 32,200 = 118,350. Equating the number 118,350 as days proved it to be 11 orbits of Saturn with just one leap day. It was also 324 years to the nearest 11 leap days. That result was quite unique for the orbits of Saturn and the solar year are at their closest point to share the same anniversary date every 324 years.

• There was a crossover where Ephraim was listed before Manasseh in the 1st census but after him in the 2nd census. That crossover was signalled in the Book of Genesis Chapter 48:14 where Jacob crossed his arms to bless the younger grandson Ephraim with his right hand while he blessed the older Manasseh with his left hand. Blessing the younger Ephraim with the right hand was against tradition and thus raised objections from the boys father Joseph. The crossover proved to be very fruitful for the half tribe of Ephraim came to 36,500 or 100 solar years. Simeon and Asher had provided the shop window clue with the solar and sidereal years that eventually led to Ephraim at 36,500.

CHAPTER 3

41

- Because of the crossover it was found necessary in the preliminary findings to highlight each tribe with a colour so as to readily trace each name as their position changed in the various biblical references. It was a surprise to find that the tribes had each been given a specific colour with regard to a breastplate in Exodus 28:15-21. It was if the scribes had also used the same colours to highlight their tables of numbers

- The numbers for Dan in the half counts were 63,550, which as days was 174 years. The tribe of Dan was noticeable by its absence from the listing of the tribes in the Book of Revelation thus provoking an interest to probe further and see if there was some reason for the omission.

- The first seven names in the Messiah time-table with Reuben, Simeon, Gad, Judah, Issachar, Zebulon, and Manasseh in sequence added up as follows:

$$45,115 + 40,750 + 43,075 + 75,550 +$$
$$59,350 + 58,950 + 42,450 = 365,240$$

That total of 365,240 in days was 1,000 years to within just two leap days. It was an incredible result but so simple to detect and it was also in that sound format of seven tribes in direct sequence.

- The totals of Ephraim, Benjamin, Asher and Naphtali at 36,500 + 40,500 + 47,450 + 49,400 = 173,850, which as days came to 476 years with just five leap days.

• Gad and Asher were from the same mother and thus formed a mini-grouping. But in the two censuses they were separated, which suggested perhaps a larger mini-grouping was being highlighted by the scribes. Indeed they were two such mini-groupings in the Messiah time-frame as follows: Nine tribes in series from Gad to Asher inclusive = 467,375, which as days was 32 laps of the special forty year cycle of Venus at 14,605.5 days. That cycle of Venus will be explained later. Seven tribes between Gad and Asher totalled 376,850 which, as days, was 87 orbits of the planet Jupiter.

• Anna the descendent of Asher was in the temple and it was the descendent of Naphtali who helped build the original temple. The two names together suggested a mini-grouping and their two half-counts in the Messiah time-frame added to 47,450 + 49,400 = 96,850, which as days were 9 orbits of Saturn.

• Continuing with the mini-grouping of Asher and Naphtali together in sequence and the presence of Simeon in the temple led to the numbers of the five tribes of Leah in the half counts to be added with Asher + Naphtali + Simeon + Reuben + Judah + Issachar + Zebulun = 376,565. The number 376,565 as days proved to be exactly 1,031 solar years. The accuracy was astounding but the second surprise with the total of those seven tribes was that it was also 35 orbits of Saturn. It again was a unique period and was at the closest possible point for the solar year and Saturn to come together. i.e. just 7 days apart in 1,031 years.

• The final result for the moment arises from the totals of Ephraim, Asher and Naphtali. Their numbers at 36,500 + 47,450 + 49,400 = 133,350, which as days was 365.172 by 365.172 or the solar year multiplied by itself. There was a slight inaccuracy but that was not the point.

Rather, that result was like a royal seal from the Hebrew's for they copied it from a much older archive of time that is still under research.

Therefore, it can be seen that the recordings of the solar years and the orbits of the planets were not just archived willy-nilly by the scribes but were formed in particular mini-groupings. So often, those mini-groupings were signposted such as with Jacob crossing his arms to favour Ephraim whose numbers in the Messiah time-frame turned out to be 36,500 or the equivalent of 100 solar years.

Those were the days, all the days, from the beginning to the end of days. The two censuses have stood through time like the pyramids, while onlookers from every generation passed by unaware of the intelligent design within their secret interior chamber. Reflect for a while on the glorious handiwork of the creators of that magnificent architectural time piece. Try to imagine how those numerical banks were conceived, designed and completed with such intricate perfection. That creation was not the only achievement made by the creators for their means of concealment stood insatiable scrutiny through thousands of years. Yet, the creators or subsequent scribes left helpful cryptic hints to prompt the faithful of a secret content. Such clues were evident at the birth of Jesus who was born in Bethlehem at the time of a census and with the statement about Rachel weeping for her children. In silence those memory banks stood on the written landscape only to be bypassed by the minds eye down through the ages. They were just two censuses of numbers, a total of unknown men buried away like mounds on a hillside that cover up the unsung casualties of war. If the words of the good book were so profound, yet malleable and all embracing, why then were the numbers perceived as being no more than rigid zombies serving a superficial role; devoid of any intelligent purpose?

The numbers in the seven burnt offerings had been encased

in seven checksums that validated their values as being original. However, with the censuses there were so many valid time measurements related to the solar year or the orbit of the planets that could have fulfilled the checksum requirements. Nevertheless, the numbers of the censuses were evaluated for such a proofing system. The tribe of Levi had been counted separately and it was likely that any overall checksum would have to take those numbers on board. But when the numbers of the tribe of Levi were examined they revealed that there was a major mistake in the biblical figures. The tribe of Levi was counted in three lots as follows:

$$7,500 + 6,200 + 8,600 = 22,000$$

That result of 22,000 listed as the total of those three numbers was an unbelievable gaffe for the correct addition totalled 22,300. Surely this mistake must have been spotted by biblical scholars throughout the centuries but yet, the error remained uncorrected. Without getting side tracked it is suffice to say that the mistake proved to be deliberate. It turned out to be a method of conveying to future generations about the use of fractions.

There was also another difference with the Levites for they were to receive no inheritance. In contrast, the other twelve tribes had that formula to divide the sum of their two totals up so as to apportion inheritance rights. Because the Levites were to receive no such inheritance it implied that the same instructions of dividing up the numbers did not apply. Therefore, it was only necessary to add the numbers of the 1st and 2nd count of the Levites to the half counts of the other twelve tribes. The correct 1st count of the Levites was 22,300 while the second count was listed as 23,000. Therefore, the combined totals of the Levites and the twelve other tribes from the Messiah time-frame were as follows:

$$22,300 + 23,000 = 45,300 + 602,640 = 647,940$$

That figure of 647,940 proved to be 1,774 years to the exact day. It was a valid checksum to prove the numbers of all the tribes as having retained their original values. The result also conformed to the pattern of solar years that were revealed in the previous analysis. In the process, that result even confirmed that the number 22,300 was intended as the correct value for the first census of the Levites.

It was an impressive result and should have been sufficient to confirm that all the numbers in the censuses of the complete thirteen tribes had retained their original values intact throughout their daunting journey in history. But, the scribes had obviously wanted to give a second proof that would convey a cast iron seal of authenticity on those sacred numbers. They included a further checksum that would prove the numbers to be days and their subsequent conversion to years to be the correct course to apply. In the earlier analysis, the burnt offerings that were made by Solomon had been interpreted to represent three periods of 1,000 years. This interpretation was supported by the reference from Nehemiah about the walls of Jerusalem that were 1,000 cubits long and were finished in 52 days. Those two numbers of 1,000 and the 52 days co-related exactly to the leap days in 1,000 years when measured with the temple calendar. The evidence seemed substantial at that point but still open to challenge. At least that was until the period of 1,000 years was found presented in the equivalent of actual days with 365,240 in the analysis above. That figure of 365,240 was unique enough to prove that the period of 1,000 years was definitely intended by the scribes. Now those biblical authors had provided a similar guarantee where they again used the walls of Jerusalem as the validation password. The secret confirmation of the years was to be revealed from the Book of Revelation.

It outlined in Chapter 21 of Revelation that the author John was shown the holy city of Jerusalem coming down out of heaven. That eternal city had a great high wall with twelve gates on which were written the names of the twelve tribes of Israel. The city, its gates and its walls were measured with a reed or rod and found to be 12,000 furlongs (stadia) in length. The names of the twelve tribes had been cited and curiously their names were actually listed in Chapter 7 of Revelation each having 12,000 of their numbers sealed. Those twelve numbers listed as 12,000 for each tribe appear to relate to the twelve signs of the Zodiac, which were cited in the earlier chapter relative to the quote from Whitrow about finite time. In Chapter 14 of Revelation an angel with a sharp sickle comes out of the temple in heaven and another angel who was in charge of the fire came out from the altar. A temple, an altar and fire together; so burnt offerings were to be expected. Even the setting was not in doubt for there was only one temple which was in the holy city of Jerusalem. The grapes of wrath were ripe enough to harvest with the sickle and were thrown into the winepress. The chapter ended as follows:

And the winepress was trodden without the city, and blood came out of the winepress, even onto the horse bridles, by the space of a thousand and six hundred furlongs. Rev. 14: 20

The measurement was without the city whose walls had previously measured 1,000 cubits. But now the measurement was not in the language of bricks and mortar but in the life line of blood. Blood that was trampled from wine and that transformation was clearly signifying the burnt offerings where the hins of wine were mingled with the slaughtered beasts. That blood line was 1,600 furlongs or stadia long.

The tribes were listed in Revelation but with a significant difference. The tribes of Joseph and Levi were now included while Dan and Ephraim were excluded. The Levites had been counted with two censuses albeit separately and their two totals were 22,300 + 23,000 = 45,300. Joseph had been represented by his two sons Manasseh and Ephraim but now the former was listed in Revelation while the latter was excluded. It would be correct therefore to slot Joseph in for Ephraim for the full tribe of Joseph would be represented because Manasseh was also listed. The tribe of Dan was not listed in the twelve tribes as cited in Revelation. The totals of the eleven tribes as listed in the Book of Revelation with respect to the Messiah time-frame were then added to the total of the undivided number of the Levites as follows:

Judah	75,550
Reuben	45,115
Gad	43,075
Asher	47,450
Naphtali	49,400
Manasseh	42,450
Simeon	40,750
Levi	45,300
Issachar	59,350
Zebulun	58,950
Joseph	36,500
Benjamin	40,500
Total	**584,390**

That total of 584,390 proved to be the equivalent of 1,600 years to the nearest 2 leap days. It co-related with the length of the life line of blood of 1,600 furlongs that was outside the city walls of Jerusalem. Previously, the 1,000 years had been listed as cubits but revealed as that very definable figure of 365,240, which was so readily recognisable as the number of days in 1,000 years. Now the totals of the tribes as listed in Revelation totalled 584,390, which as days was the equivalent of 1,600 years. In both cases there was an error of two leap days.

Because ten of the totals of each tribe had ended with a zero the error of two days was understandable. But those measurements were so profound it was likely that the scribes had factored in those two days in some format. They did and with the highest profile that could be ordained. The Israelites set out on their long journey and only the Levites were allowed to carry the tabernacle that housed the Ark of the Covenant. A cloud descended on the tabernacle and while it lasted the Israelites could not set out from the camp. The cloud effectively controlled the movements of the tribes often covering the tabernacle by day and with the appearance of fire by night. The scribes eventually got to the point where they stated:

Or whether it were two days, or a month, or a year, that the cloud tarried upon the tabernacle, remaining thereon, the children of Israel abode in their tents, and journeyed not: but when it was taken up , they journeyed. Numbers 9:22

There are only three natural time periods which are the solar day, lunar month and solar year. All three periods are contained in the citation above thus prompting the significance of time and how it is measured. In fact, that profound statement with its time related dimension was confirming the truth; that time was the real issue. To reinforce this view, there were just two days specifically listed and not one or five, eight or ten. Therefore, for two days the twelve tribes would have stayed in their tents waiting for the cloud to lift so that the Levites could carry the tabernacle. All thirteen tribes had just been counted and would follow the Ark as would their descendants in the second census almost thirty

nine years later. The totals from the two censuses, excluding Dan, as reckoned for the Messiah time-frame together with the Levites added up to 584,390, which was 2 days longer than 1,600 years. The circuitry linking all the events back to the two days was a testament in itself that the cloud had been lifted to confirm the checksum result of 1,600 years to the very day. Thus, the numbers of days disguised as the numbers of the tribes had been validated by two separate check sum results. The first involved the numbers of the twelve tribes plus the Levites and proved to be 1,774 years to the exact day. The second checksum was with eleven tribes and the Levites (excluding Dan) and it proved to be the same number in years as the numbered length of the blood line around the city walls of Jerusalem at 1,600.

The secret vault of time was potent with many unusual measurements of lengthy periods which will be shown to serve a very definite purpose. It will be necessary to analyse the function of those time periods and set them out as a highway from beginning to end. The notion of a highway was prompted in Chapter 3 of Luke's Gospel where John, who was six months older than Jesus, referred to making straight a pathway through the desert. It was not the first such reference to making straight a way in the desert for it also had been suggested by Isaiah as follows:

"The voice of him that crieth in the wilderness, prepare ye the way of the Lord, and make straight in the desert a highway for our God." Isaiah 40 3

Those two statements relative to John and Isaiah were pointing in the direction of the desert wilderness where the tribes had travelled in a semi-circle. In the earlier quote from Isaiah, he had referred to sitting on the circle of the earth. The shape of an arc was evident in that peculiar language and as such, the greater dome of the sky above was perhaps being spiritually compassed in the receptive mind. In that regard, the numbers of the twelve tribes in the inner Messiah time-frame would now provide that highway through time for the Lord. In the next chapter, the starting point of where the time measurements began in the Bible will be set out. It will be followed with an outline of seven separate time line measurements that have come to light ranging from Abraham, Isaac, Jacob and Solomon down to the birth, ministry and final passion of Jesus at the end of days.

The Wailing Wall

CHAPTER 4

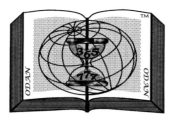

THE TEMPLE SCROLL

There were seven burnt offerings whose numbers were verified as being original by seven checksums. The temple calendar had the potential to open up many mysterious doors automatically for measuring the history of the Bible. It appeared that from the reign of King Hezekiah to the sudden death of Josiah was the epicentre, for several fundamental aspects of the temple calendar stemmed from that period. One such indelible example was found charted in that era where it was noticeable that Hezekiah reigned for 29 years, his son Manasseh for 55 years, Amon for 2 years and Josiah for 31 years. The period from the beginning of the reign of King Hezekiah to the sudden death of his great grandson Josiah in years was as follows:

$$29 + 55 + 2 + 31 = 117 \text{ years}$$

The scribes had seemingly written the script as a path to follow for it was that special period of 117 years or its equivalent of 55 temple years. It was such an important period of the temple calendar to encounter and it also spanned that crisis time from the fall of Israel to the death of Josiah.

The period of 117 years ended when King Josiah was killed by an Egyptian arrow after he went into battle against Pharaoh's army. The biblical commentary on the rule of the previous kings suddenly came to a stop with the death of Josiah in 608 BCE as if the arrow had etched a full stop target in blood. But that arrow came from Egypt and Isaiah's statement about using tables also related to dealing with the Egyptians. The hunch was to follow the origins of the arrow and trace back in time from Josiah to earlier events in Egypt. To support that line of reasoning there was a quote stating that not since Moses was there such an exemplarily leader like Josiah and that he held the biggest Passover feast for generations. That made a clear linkage between Josiah and Moses and the reference to Pharaoh reinforced that bond. But, there was even further links where, at the time of Josiah, a sacred scroll was found hidden in the temple. That scroll was referred to as the Torah of Moses and scholars believe it may have been the book of Deuteronomy. From the results of these research findings, it would appear that the book contained the contents that were dictated by Moses as outlined at the end of the Book of Deuteronomy. It would now seem that those contents were likely to have been the details of the temple calendar. It thus seemed logical to name this recent discovery, The Temple Calendar.

The clues were pointing in the direction of Moses so it was necessary to follow those signposts and trace back in time through the Bible to the Exodus. The dating back in time from Josiah would likely have begun in his 18th year circa 620 BCE when the temple scroll was found and the greatest Passover for years was celebrated. The journey went back to the time of Moses and those burnt offerings in Chapters 29 and 28 of the Book of Numbers. There were three such offerings in Chapters 29 that contained those numbers of 117. The trail then continued back to Chapter 28 of Numbers where three deciphered periods of 217 years was encountered. The logical sequence of the trail where 117 as years was first encountered and it was followed by 217 as years, which

Killingbeck Cemetary, Leeds

proved to be like a sequence that complemented the profile of dating back in time.

The totals of all those translated periods in Chapter 29 and 28 of the Book of Numbers were as follows:

	Years	Leap days		Years	Leap Days
Chapter 29	117	- 1 ⅔	Chapter 28	217	+ 3 ½
	117	- 1 ⅔		217	+ 3 ½
	117	- 1 ⅔		217	+ 3 ½
Total =	351 Years	-5 days	Total =	651 years	+ 10 ½ days

The two results of 351 and 651 gave a combined total of 1,002 years. An academic supervisor would ask the student to demonstrate the tangible supporting evidence to justify adding up those numbers as periods of time. To that end the patterns of two by two were again evident. Just as in the earlier findings, the supporting evidence of matching leap days to fractions was there to reinforce these deductions. Those fractions were included in the table above. The totals of the leap days for three periods of 117 years was - 1 ⅔ x 3 = - 5 days while the totals for three periods of 217 years was + 3 ½ x 3 = + 10 ½ days. The combined total thus was − 5 + 10 ½ = + 5 ½ days. Interestingly, the total of the fractions in those combined chapters of 28 and 29 of the Book of Numbers added up to 5 1/10, which matched up very favourably with the 5 ½ leap days. Note 13 Thus, those fractions having been equal to the leap days reinforced the exercise of dating back in time with the three periods of 117 and 217 years.

The main subject of superimposing the biblical period of thrice 117 and 217 years, totalling 1,002 years from King Josiah back in time could now take place. Our conventional dating system decrees that such a journey back in time must conform to the BCE dating method. Therefore, the period from the 18th year of Josiah in 620 BCE (When the scroll was found and the Passover held) led back through 1,002 years in history to circa 1,622 BCE. It would soon transpire that the Biblical authors had a grand plan in place for the period of casting back from Josiah by 1,002 years led back to Abraham. The conventional dating of the Bible was about to be rewritten.

The exercise of dating back in time was signalled to us by Isaiah with the episode of turning the clock back in time and again the activity was with King Hezekiah. Isaiah had arranged for the clock of Ahaz to go back by 10 degrees so that Hezekiah, who was dying, lived for another 15 years. That was no ordinary clock for if 10 degrees represented 15 years then the full 360 degrees of the clock would amount to 540 years. Hezekiah had to wait three days before the miracle took effect, which suggested three periods of 540 years. That added up to 1,620 years. It was a surprise result particularly in the light of the earlier exercise where counting back 1,002 years from Josiah had led to almost the same period with 1,622 BCE. It appeared that Isaiah had gone to great numerical lengths to deliberately define the period of 1,620 years albeit in a mathematical formula. Hezekiah also referred to the clock going forward as a natural state so the possibility of the remaining part of 620 years (1,622 -1,002 = 620) being cast forward in time was strongly prompted. That position was verified in the Book by Josephus where there was a commentary on the clock of Ahaz also going forward. The projection forward in time from Josiah would lead exactly to the very beginning of the AD era at the birth of Jesus. What had come to light would soon prove to be the greatest long term strategic planning exercise in human history. Isaiah et al were forecasting the future and had mapped out the time line from their era in 608 -740 BCE to the birth of the Messiah on a calendar system.

CHAPTER 5

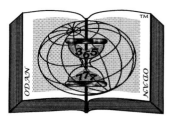

SEVEN SACRED TIME PERIODS

THE FIRST BIBLICAL TIME PERIOD FROM LUKE'S GENEALOGY

The clues to the first time-line measurement were found at the beginning of Chapter 3 of Luke's Gospel where it referred to the reign of Tiberius and stated that Jesus was about 30 years old at that time. That sentence about Jesus led directly into a very long genealogy that dated back through the Bible to David onto Jacob, Isaac and Abraham, then onto Adam as the 76th in line. Finally, God was listed as the 77th and last in line. It was noticed that the name Levi appeared twice in Luke's genealogy. The Levites were 30 years old when they began their ministry and of course the genealogy began by stating that Jesus was about 30 years old. David was 30 years old when he was made king and three of the descendants of Noah were 30 years old when they became fathers. Therefore, the most common known age bond throughout Luke's genealogy was the period of 30 years. It seemed so logical that all of the people named in the genealogy were also to be apportioned the age of 30 years just as with the Levites when they began their ministry. Note 14 The next step was to multiply the generations by 30 years with the 56 generations back to Abraham and that gave the vast period of 1,680 years. There was a note of caution required for there were errors with certain historical names in Luke's genealogy which would have to be addressed.

That exercise of allotting the period of 30 years for each generation might raise many eyebrows. But, there was the Messiah time-frame now on hand to reinforce that lengthy period from the birth of Isaac to Jesus when he was 30 years of age. The total of the Messiah time-frame comprising of the numbers of the twelve tribes of Israel was 602,640 days, which was nine days short of 1,650 years. That period of 1,650 years matched up with the period from Isaac to Jesus, as can be discerned from Luke's genealogy. Even the nine days of a shortfall was accounted for because the time-frame took on board the circumcision of Isaac on the eight day after he was born. Therefore, the first lane of the Lord's highway in time had been re-constructed, first from Luke's genealogy and secondly from the Messiah time-frame.

THE SECOND BIBLICAL TIME PERIOD FROM MATHEW'S GENEALOGY

The clue to the second time measurement was in Mathew's Gospel with a genealogy which listed the names of the descendants from Abraham down to Jesus. It stated that there were 42 generations but ironically only 41 names were listed though David was cited twice. The same principle as with Luke's genealogy of assigning a set period for each generation would have to apply. That set period could not be the same at 30 years and simple arithmetic determined that 40 years was the prime candidate.

There was ample support for the period of 40 years for David, Solomon and many other biblical rulers reigned for that length of time. By applying the 40 years to each generation from Abraham to Jesus the length of the period for the stated 42 generations was 1,680 years. That was the same result as with the genealogy in Luke's Gospel. There were also omissions of historical names in Mathew's genealogy and those were Ahziah, Joash and Omaziah. However, with the benefit of the time measurement it would now appear that those omissions were deliberately intended. It facilitated making the period from Abraham to Jesus 1,680 years for both Mathew's and Luke's genealogy.

From the analyses of the two censuses above it was possible to reinforce that method of measuring time in periods of 40 years. In the first census the totals of Leah's sons added up to 292,200, which as days was 800 years to within six leap days. That number of 292,200 was recognisable, for it was also in days the length of one hundred 'octaeteris,' a period which was encountered earlier in the checksums of the burnt offerings. By equating the 800 years to Mathew's genealogy it would account for twenty periods of 40 years. Therefore, that unique total of the numbers of Leah's sons when presented as days provided the support for almost half the journey of the 40 year periods in Mathew's genealogy. From the analysis of the censuses above a further complimentary measurement will be outlined shortly to cement the period of 40 years as a separate parallel time-line of the Lord's highway.

A Divining Rod

There was a something significant that came to light with periods of 30 and 40 years respectively as a set age for each genealogy. They both added up to 70 years. The two genealogies had the same names from Abraham to David but then they were split like a great divining rod. The two arms of the genealogy then stretched out in parallel all the way from David to Jesus. David was 30 years when he became King and then reigned for 40 years so his two ages combine to make up the 70 years. It appeared that David's ages were the prototype for the two genealogies. Those mysterious quotes from Jeremiah and Daniel about the precious period of 70 years now took on a purposeful value. Note 15 It also provided a real purpose for the inclusion of the number 70 in the burnt offerings that were made by Ezra. In that offering the 70 was seen as the odd one out.

To draw the image of a divining rod as the shape of the two genealogies would be just a metaphorical observation were it not for the noticeable clues left for us to follow. Those first such clue was evident in the Book of Isaiah where it was stated as follows:

And there shall come forth a rod out of the stem of Jesse, and a branch shall grow out of his roots. Is. 11:1

That statement about a rod out of the stem of Jesse was the subject of much debate by biblical scholars and was viewed as pointing to Jesus. The associated messages in the same chapter were of teaching equity for the meek and so the link to Jesus was understandable. But in the context of these findings the rod signified the shape of the two genealogies. It was also possible that the rod was synonymous with the staff that the patriarchs carried. There was strong supporting evidence for those observations and it was again to be found with Isaiah as follows:

As if the rod could shake itself against those that lift it up, or as if the staff should lift up itself, as if it were no wood. Is. 10: 15

The words of the Bible can often be ambiguous but that quote was plain speaking. A divining rod shakes violently against the person who holds it when they walk over a natural spring thus revealing the presence of water trapped below ground. Indeed, the forked rod sometimes raises itself upwards but mostly it twists towards the ground and draws on the strength of the two arms of the person holding it. It can even have such force that the person is drawn to their knees. Isaiah had made it simple to equate the rod with the staff for he wrote it into the quote itself. He even indicated the presence of some greater force where he referred to the mysterious actions of the rod and staff and observed, *as if they were no wood.*

The evidence was fairly clear cut and strongly suggested that the rod out of the stem of Jesse was describing the shape of the diving rod with respect to the two genealogies. The branch that grew out of its roots began with David where his two ages split into the periods of 30 and 40 years. The names on the family tree of that branch were David's two sons Nathan and Solomon and from them the blood line stretched all the way down to Jesus. On the other end the stem stretched all the way back to Isaac and Abraham. If the image of a divining rod was correct then it would be expected to find a spring well at the end of the stem. That brought the research back to the Book of Genesis where springs were so highly profiled that they were even included in a treaty. Indeed, those wells were almost as vibrant to observe as 'Old Faithful' in Yellowstone National Park. That was where Abraham and Isaac were both involved in digging wells. Note 16

CHAPTER 5

65

Of course, to dig wells they have first to be divined. So the ability to divine wells with a forked rod was inherent at the end of the stem. Thus, that supernatural ability of dousing by the first two patriarchs conferred a divine mantle over the two genealogies.

The scribes made the linkage with the divining rod and the temple calendar more watertight when the included the episode in a treaty between Abraham and King Abimelech at a place that was then named Beersheba. Abraham brought cattle and sheep and he gave Abimelech seven lambs for the King in recognition that he (Abraham) had dug those wells. The principle of the seven lambs for the burnt offering sacrifices and the linkage with the divining rod was thus instigated in that treaty. Some years later the episode with the wells was repeated between Isaac and Abimelech. Isaac's live stock grew in number so the Philistines filled the wells to stop the herds from watering themselves. It outlined that Isaac had to re-dig the wells and, of course, in sandy terrain he would have had to locate them first by a diving rod. The next in line was Jacob who openly displayed the powers of the divining rod when he spiked the drinking and breeding habits of his uncle Labans' animals with a forked stick. The reference to a rod or staff together with water was synonymous with the characters that walked the divine time line. e.g. Moses struck a rock with his rod and water gushed out was a perfect clue.

The comparisons between the events at the two ends of the story were sufficient to show that there was a tangible link between the two scenes. It is not intended to outline the details surrounding the birth of Jesus but to list the similarities between both ends of the story as follows:

The Alpha in the beginning	The Omega at the end
The aged Abraham and Sarah	The aged Zachary and Elizabeth
Three men from God pay a visit	Three wise men pay a visit
Sarah sleeps with Pharaoh and King Abimelech who were perceived as Gods	The angel Gabriel intercedes from on high with Elizabeth and Mary
Twins are born to Rebecca and Isaac	Two boys are born to Elizabeth and Mary
Rachel died in childbirth delivering Benjamin in Bethlehem	Jesus was born at Bethlehem
Jacob was the son of Isaac and Joseph his grandson	Joseph was the step father of Jesus and Jacob his step grandfather
A heavenly phenomena at the birth of Abraham with bright stars in the sky(Book of Jasher)	That story of the bright star at Bethlehem at the birth of Jesus.
The King at the time of Abraham orders all new born males to be killed (Jasher)	King Herod ordered all new born males to be killed at the time of Jesus
Abraham makes a covenant with King Abimelech and gives him seven lambs from his flock. (Burnt Offering, 777)	The shepherds were minding their flock and came to adore Jesus

It was as if an SOS signal had been transmitted at the beginning with Abraham, Isaac, and Jacob and its images arrived intact some 1,600 years later to be re-televised at the birth of Jesus and John. The computations with two genealogies had now forged a direct time linkage between those two eras.

THE THIRD BIBLICAL TIME PERIOD FROM SOLOMON TO JESUS

Dating back in time from Josiah with the finding of the temple scroll in Circe 620 BCE went back to the reign of King Solomon. As per the earlier findings in Chapter 4, the first three periods would be 117 + 117 + 117 years = 351 years. Adding 351 years to 620 BCE led back to 971 BCE. It was a remarkable result for Solomon made those three burnt offerings of 1,000 bullocks, 1,000 rams and 1,000 lambs on the morning after his father David had died. That was in the historical year of 971 BCE. And this research has outlined that those burnt offerings involving the number 1,000 were intended to signal a similar period in years. One such period of 1,000 years would thus run from Solomon to Jesus. (According to Josephus P270, the man of God many centuries before Josiah had prophesied a period of 361 years to Josiah as compared to the 351 years shown above.)

Fast forwarding in time by 1,000 years from the time when Solomon became king in 971BC would measure out to 29CE, which notably was about the time when Jesus began to preach. It outlined in Luke's Gospel that Jesus began to preach in the 15th year of the reign of Tiberius which is known to be the year 29CE. It seemed a solid anchor of time to date the timing of the biblical calendar against civil time for it took on board an actual date in the Julian calendar of the mighty Roman Empire. It was remarkable how this new dating system with the temple calendar fitted in precisely with the conventional biblical timeline relative to Solomon being made king and the 1,000 years to 29AD.

The Messiah time-frame had produced the supporting period of 1,650 years in days to prove that the application of Luke's genealogy with the 30 years per generation was correct. Now, that Messiah time-frame would be to the forefront again for it encap

The Wall of Jerusalem

sulated the period of 1,000 years from Solomon to Jesus. In the analysis above the additions of the first seven tribes in that inner sanctuary of the censuses had totalled up as follows:

Reuben + Simeon + Gad + Judah + Issachar + Zebulon + Manasseh

45,115 + 40,750 + 43,075 + 75,550 + 59,350 + 58,950 + 42,450
= 365,240

That total of 365,240 in days was 1,000 years to within just two leap days. The scribes had provided the perfect result with skilful planning. Solomon made the burnt offerings that contained 1,000 of each animal and later, Nehemiah built the walls of Jerusalem 1,000 cubits long. Those were the cryptic clues. But finally, the scribes had taken the gloves off and provided the real period of 1,000 years with its very recognisable number of 365,240 days.

There was even another surprise in store for the display of 365,240 as days in the Messiah time-frame meant that before the figures were halved, there was twice that figure. It meant that the totals of the first seven tribes in the two censuses added up to 730,480, which as days was 2,000 years. Solomon had made a burnt offering that totalled 3,000 animals in all and now matching that figure in the computations of the two censuses was 730,480 + 365,240, which was the equivalent of 3,000 years.

Many things were now falling into place and especially the application of that period of 1,000 years to the Messiah time-frame served a real purpose. That result with 1,000 years had in fact divided the Messiah time-frame into two parts, the other section being 650 years with just five leap days. It was now possible to go even further and utilise the very words of the Bible to build in more of the time-frame. It stated in the first Book of Kings that:

*And it came to pass in the four hundred and eightieth year after the
children of Israel were come out of the land of Egypt, in the fourt
year of Solomon's reign over Israel, in the month of Zif, which is the
second month, that he began to build the house of the Lord.*
1Kings Chapter 6:1

By subtracting four years from the period of 480 years it resulted in the period of 476 years, which was when Solomon began
to reign. The 480 year period had perplexed biblical scholars for
thousands of years for it was totally at odds with the statement in
the Book of Exodus, which outlined that the Israelites were 430
years in Egypt to the very day. At long last, it was now possible
to verify which one of those periods was the correct one. From
the analyses of the Messiah time-frame four of the numbers from
the remaining names that followed the 1,000 year period were
as follows:

Ephraim + Benjamin + Asher   + Naphtali

36,500 + 40,500 + 47,450 + 49,400   = 173,850

That number of 173,850 as days was 476 years with just five
leap days. Yes, it was the equivalent to the period of 476 years
that was inherent from the statement relative to Solomon building the temple. The one drawback was that it derived from the
tribes of Ephraim and Benjamin together and then skipped Dan
to conclude with the totals of Asher and Naphtali. It would have
been all the more spectacular if the result had derived from those
four tribes all in sequence after the other seven tribes that totalled
1,000 years.

In so many of the revelations so far, there was often an inner
twist to such an outcome. However, it was felt that in this case
that it had not been possible for the scribes to factor in those four

tribes in sequence because it would disturb so many other mini-groupings within the Messiah time-frame. It was evident that finding the result of 476 (480 - 4 = 476) years in the time-frame to match up with when Solomon began his reign relative to the timing of the Exodus was not likely to be an unbelievable coincidence. After all, there were just five tribes involved in that last part of the time-line and the first and last two were separated by the tribe of Dan. Nevertheless, the scribes seemingly were anxious that such an important period of 476 years should not be suspect for it was the correct period. Unlike the 480 years, the 430 years was devised to satisfy the make-believe story. In the Book of Revelation, the tribe of Dan was excluded from a listing of the twelve tribes and was replaced by Levi. Because the tribe of Levi was not to be counted with the other tribes and Dan no longer featured in the list, it meant that those four tribes of Ephraim, Benjamin, Asher and Naphtali were in reality, all in sequence as pertinent numbers to be counted. Those numbers proved to be the equivalent of the 476 years, which was the period outlined in the Bible, from the Exodus out of Egypt to the year when Solomon began his reign.

THE MAGIC SPELL OF TEMPLE TIME

There was one more source of biblical literature to be examined with respect to the heavens and that was with the Dead Sea Scrolls. In that regard, the course of the luminaries appeared to have been of special interest to the Israelites relative to time keeping as VanderKam outlined:

"The calendars, with their unalterable rhythms, also expressed the theological or philosophical conviction that the courses of the luminaries, and the cycles of festivals and priestly duties operated in

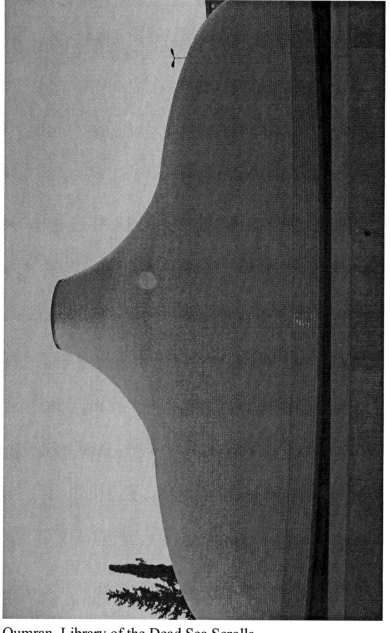

Qumran, Library of the Dead Sea Scrolls

a cosmic harmony imposed upon them by the creator God himself."
Vanderkam P 112

There was no evidence given by VanderKam of finding real examples in the Qumran texts or how the luminaries operated in cosmic harmony with the cycles of festivals. But the scribes had extended the scope of their work to cover remarkable long stretches of time with what VanderKam called literal chronologies to encase all or part of history.

Those chronologies from Mathew's and Luke's Gospels had encased 1,680 of history so the findings from the research had brought those facts to life. The reference by VanderKam to the course of the luminaries was a further spotlight on the heavens but again there was no mathematical evidence from the scrolls to suggest those references were anything more than aspirations. That was until the regular orbits of Saturn, Jupiter, Venus and the solar and lunar years had been revealed above in the analysis of the censuses of the tribes. But there was even more creative accounting by the scribes to be considered, which would bring those luminaries under the spell of the temple calendar.

The Israelites were sometimes unfaithful and tried to put stumbling blocks in the way of Moses. There were separate scenes where 250, 24,000, 14,700 died for being unfaithful. Another ten of the men who were sent spying by Moses died of the plague, two Rubenites were swallowed up by the earth; one man was stoned to death while a man was lanced for having sex with a foreigner. Those individual men totalled 14 in all. But even before the first census, 3,000 men were slain on the orders of Moses for worshipping the golden calf. Note 17 Those biblical events proved to be concocted stories to facilitate the introduction of specific numbers that would soon serve to bridge the gap between linear and orbital time.

The Fourth Biblical Time Period: The Saviour of Israel

The presence of the orbits of the three main planets of Jupiter, Saturn and Venus was outlined above in the analysis of the Messiah time-frame. However, it was necessary to demonstrate the uniqueness of those discoveries relative to particular orbits of those planets being recorded by the scribes. It is now possible to show that those recorded cycles were specifically selected because the orbits of the relevant planets were closest to being in harmony with particular periods of solar years. The first example arises in the overall context of the census where 250 men were consumed by an earthquake or by fire. It was noticed that the figure of those 250 men was again repeated where they were listed with the second census. Taking that repeat as a clue the computations were carried out and the number 250 was deducted from the first census for that was implied. The instructions from Moses to add the two totals of the censuses and then halve them were performed and the result was as follows:

$$603{,}550 - 250 = 603{,}300 + 601{,}730 = 1.205{,}030 \div 2 = 602{,}515$$

The outcome of adding the modified first census to the second census and half the resultant total was 602,515. It was eureka for that number as days proved to be 56 orbits of Saturn to the exact day. The halo had been lifted off the numerical jigsaw to reveal that the scribes had devised the equation to harmonise 56 orbits of Saturn with the totals of the Messiah time-frame.

The real significance of the result was that from Luke's genealogy, time would have measured out 55 periods of 30 years to 1,650 years, which was practically the same as the totals as 602,640 days of the Messiah time-frame. Within the same period, 56 orbits of Saturn would occur, i.e. the orbit of Saturn at 29 years 167 days by 56 times = 1,649 years 231 days. Those numbers were an earthly concept while the orbit of Saturn above was a heavenly occurrence. The scribes had crossed a divine threshold for now they had captured Saturn within their magical numbers. It required just a simple correction process to synchronise those 56 orbits of Saturn with 1,650 solar years for both clocks to be in harmony. And it was all achieved by a numbering system.

One swallow does not make a summer so it was necessary to find more supporting examples to prove that the most notable orbit of Saturn, which would be in closest harmony with periods of solar years was recorded by the scribes. A simulation exercise was carried out to establish the closest intersection points between Saturn and the solar year in the space of 1,650 years. The four closest intersections were as follows:

- After 324 years to within 12 ¾ days.
- After 707 years to within 5 ⅔ days.
- After 1,031 years to within 7 days.
- After 1,414 years to within 10 2/5 days.

The true test would be to find those periods as listed when Saturn was in cosmic harmony with multiples of the solar year. The censuses were examined for evidence of the orbits of Saturn together with the solar years. In the first census, the totals of the numbers of Ephraim, Manasseh and Gad added up at 40,500 + 32,200 + 45,650 = 118,350. Equating the number 118,350 as days proved it to be 11 orbits of Saturn with just one leap day. It was also 324 years to the nearest 11 ½ leap days.

It was a spectacular result so the examination continued and progressed to the Messiah time-frame where the biggest rewards were found. The findings with the solar year element will be outlined first. Those results comprised of various combinations of the numbers of each tribe that added up evenly or to within three leap days of particular periods as follows:

Solar years to the exact day: 375, 392, 1,031 years
Solar years with one leap day: 707, 1,205 years
Solar years with two to three leap days: 441, 460, 549, 566, 646, 676, 1,000 years

The Halo of Saturn

There were possibly other combinations yet to be formed. The results with respect to Saturn being in closest harmony with the solar year were as follows:

- Naphtali + Gad + Asher + Issachar + Zebulun = 258,225
  That total of 258,225 proved to be 707 years to within one leap day and of course it was also 24 orbits of Saturn. To make the finding even more profound those five names were not just chosen at random but were all laid out in sequence relative to the order of their birth.

- Reuben + Judah + Issachar + Zebulun + Simeon + Asher + Naphtali = 376,565. That number when transfigured to days proved to be 35 orbits of Saturn with just seven leap days. But 376,565 as days proved to be exactly 1,031 solar years to the very day. The first five names were all the sons of Leah thus giving the result the added dimension of a significant partial mini-grouping.

Thus, the three periods of 324, 707 and 1,031 years outlined above had been inserted by the scribes and because they were the periods that Saturn and the Solar year were closest together, it made the findings truly unique.

It was conclusive therefore that Saturn, which was known as the saviour of Israel, was being tracked so precisely. History was being re-written for those results with Saturn were unveiled from the two alleged censuses that were inserted in the Bible at least 2,500 years ago. The real scene of the Exodus had proved to be a stage managed production to carry an Ark full with the numbers of time through the pages of the Bible. That trek through the wilderness was essentially, the embodiment of the highway through this life while the Promised Land of milk and honey had that spiritual dimension of the afterlife. Saturn, the saviour of Israel, with its spectacular halo would eventually be symbolised with an angelic aura to adorn Christ and sainthood.

THE FIFTH BIBLICAL TIME PERIOD:
THE MORNING STAR

It was conceivable that the scribes had also factored in the orbit of Venus in parallel with the 40 year time span relative to Mathew's genealogy. In that regard the open salver was again with Isaiah where he referred to the morning star as follows:

"How art thou fallen from heaven O Lucifer, son of the morning! How art thou cut down to the ground." Is. 14:12

The 'son of the morning' was translated as 'the morning star' meaning the planet Venus by the Gideon Bible. Being cut down to the ground suggested that Venus had also being grounded by the earthly numbers. The reference to Venus was evident also in the Book of Revelation as follows:

"I am the root and the offspring of David, and the bright and morning star." Rev. 22:16

The bright morning star of the planet Venus was directly linked by the scribes with David and his off spring who was Solomon. Both those kings reigned for forty years and peculiarly, Venus follows a particular path through the heavens which sees it return to the same position in the sky every forty years. The actual cycle is 14,605.5 days long, which is just a four day shortfall from the exact anniversary date of 40 years.

The censuses were then examined for evidence of the 40 year cycle of Venus and surprisingly, the answer was relatively easy to find. All the five tribes of Leah's sons in the first census, which also were the first names in sequence, added up to 292,200. That figure of 292,200 as days equated to 800 years to within six leap days. That number of 292,200 was recognisable for it was also, in days, the length of one hundred 'octaeteris,' a period which was encountered earlier in the checksums of the burnt offerings. In that lengthy period of 800 years the special cycle of Venus of 14,605.5 days fell short by 84 leap days.

The Messiah time-frame was then examined to see if multiple periods of that special 14,605.5 day cycle of Venus were factored in by the scribes. Gad and Asher were a mini-grouping because they both were sons of the maid servant Zilpah. It was noticed that Gad and Asher were separated in the two censuses as if they were intended to form a larger grouping of nine tribes in direct sequence. The totals of those nine tribes added up as follows:

**Gad + Judah + Issachar + Zebulun + Manasseh
+ Ephraim + Benjamin + Dan + Asher = 467,375**

That total proved to be the equivalent of 32 laps of that lengthy special cycle of 14,605.5 days of the planet Venus. The result fell short of 1,280 years by 134 ½ leap days. Therefore, the scribes had included two examples in the censuses to show that the special orbit of Venus at 14,605.5 days was indeed recorded by them.

The research then re-focussed on the numbers of the tribes because there was something peculiar about one of the group of men that died from the plague. In that regard, the group of men numbering 14,700 soon proved to be the key to an unusual balancing act. That number of 14,700, if applied as days, was 90 days longer than 40 years. It was not expected to find a number that translated to exactly 40 years but yet that figure of 14,700 was taunting providence with its close proximity to that period. There was a second group of men numbering 24,000 who also died of the plague. That was two groups of numbers that related to the plague and as such it seemed like an invitation to carry out a similar computation exercise as pertained in the earlier example with Saturn. Therefore, the two totals of the men that died of the plague were then subtracted from the 1st census as follows:

$$603,550 - 14,700 - 24,000 = 564,850$$

This new total of 564,850 for the 1st census was then added to the 2nd census of 601,730 and the total divided as follows:

$$564,850 + 601,730 = 1,166,580 \div 2 = 583,290$$

That number of 583,290 when applied as days proved to be 1,597 years with just one leap day to be added. To find that result of 1,597 solar years was an endorsement of being on a correct path, but to where? It subsequently turned out to be one part of an equation relative to multiples of the solar year being in harmony with Venus. The other part of the equation was like a numerical bridge for it completed that harmonious relationship between Venus and that new total of 1,597 solar years.

The orbit of Venus around the sun is 224.7 days long. But Venus also follows a particular path through the heavens which is known as its synodic period. That synodic period is the time required for Venus to return to the same position relative to the Sun as seen by an observer on Earth and it is 583.9211 days long. The principle of returning to the same anniversary date was thus synonymous with the synodic period of Venus. It was plausible that multiple orbits of the synodic period were perhaps the other part of the equation to harmonise the planet Venus with 1,597 solar years of 583,290 days approx. (1 leap day) From the ensuing computations it was found that 999 synodic periods came to 583,337.16 days, which was 47 days greater than 1,597 solar years. That difference of 47 days did not create an ideal harmonious relationship with multiples of the solar year. But it was the closest point that could be achieved with the period of 1,597 years. It was the right formula on the right road leading to a unique numerical riddle. The solution to the riddle was to accept those 47 days as a bridge between 1,597 years and 999 synodic periods totalling 583,337.16 days. Thereafter, the new total of 583,337.16 days would be converted back to the numbers involved in the 1ˢᵗ census to see how it would reflect on the number 14,700, which was the equivalent to a time period of 40 years and 3 months. The computations were as follows:

583,337.16 x 2 = 1,166,674.2 − 601,730 (2nd census) = 564,944.2

Add on the 24,000 as follows: 564,944.2 + 24,000 = 588,944.2

The 1ˢᵗ census was 603,550 so the final part of the computations was as follows:

603,550 − 588,944.2 = 14,605.8

The conversion produced an astounding result for 14,605.8 as days were 65 orbits of Venus around the sun. i.e. 224.7 × 65 = 14,605.5 days. It was just four days short of being in harmony with 40 solar years.

Many of the findings in this groundbreaking research had produced results that had that eureka factor and this example with Venus even excelled that instantaneous expression. In the previous examples with Saturn and Jupiter, their orbits in years were lengthy periods and thus rarely intersected with the solar year. In contrast, those two different cycles with Venus were relatively short periods and both intersected with the solar year every 8 years. Therefore, to produce a credible result with Venus it would require a very distinctive outcome to prove it was factored into an equation by those ancient scribes. Otherwise, some result could be construed as just multiples of eight years. But could it be imagined that the scribes would provide the perfect balance between the two different orbits of Venus to confirm the issue. At one side of the formula was 999 cycles of the synodic period while at the other side there was 65 cycles of the regular orbit of 224.7 days. The quest was for that figure of 14,605.5 days, for it would have been the ultimate parallel cosmic figure that ran alongside the 40 year period relative to Mathew's genealogy. That expectation was fuelled by the reference in the Book of Revelation to the morning star and its linkage to David and Solomon. The common linkage between all three was the period of 40 years. What the scribes had served up was the exact harmonious result with those 65 orbits of Venus at 14,605.5 days mirroring 40 years. And the prime period of 40 years was laid by the journey through the wilderness. Moreover, the same principal formula with the numbers of the two censuses had applied to both Saturn and Venus with the only difference being the numbers of the men that died.

The result illustrated a marvellous balancing act and brought to mind the scene with the writing on the wall where Daniel referred to being weighed in the balances. In the reference, Daniel interpreted the ghostly writing for the king but looking at the words he spoke suggested he was spelling out the message of time and the kingdom had a heavenly dimension, particularly with regard to Venus. His interpretation was that:

"God had numbered the days of your reign, you have been weighed in the scales, your kingdom is divided." Dan 5:26:27:28

The days of both orbits of Venus were numbered. Both were divided from each other but weighed in the balances with that unique formula in time. The window dressing provided the setting where the king was with a 1,000 (nobles), called out the astrologers and diviners, and referred to the third highest ruler in the kingdom. The third highest ruler as seen by an astrologer may have been the planet Venus.

THE SIXTH BIBLICAL TIME PERIOD: THE ANOINTING OF KINGS

The whole episode of measuring time was presented as a biblical story, which was cast back in time to begin with Abraham, Isaac etc. and forecast down to the arrival of Jesus. That storyteller led us to believe that the episode began when three men from God visited Abraham who was sitting under the oak trees at Marme. The oak was the earthly symbol of the planet Jupiter and in turn that planet was revered and associated with the anointing of kings. To compliment the regal status, Sarai's name was changed to Sarah meaning princess. She had an interlude with a King called Abimelech, which was a Semitic name meaning 'father of the king.' Abraham was promised a family lineage and the oak with its annual rings of growth symbolised a family tree. The inner tree rings are also a natural way of counting the years. From all those clues it seemed likely that the cycle of the regal planet of Jupiter would be as numbered by the scribes in their tables of figures.

The results of the analysis proved it had been tracked and recorded in those numbers of the 1st censuses of the twelve tribes. The equation had a double outcome that made it all the more spectacular. Prior to the 1st census, about 3,000 men were slain because of idolatry with the golden calf. Therefore, the 1st census of 603,550 plus the 3,000 added up to 606,550, which would have been the alleged number that came out of Egypt. That figure as days proved to be 140 orbits of Jupiter to within just 12 leap days. From such a positive beginning the totals of the numbers of the 1st census were adjusted to take account of all the man-days lost for bad behaviour and the equation was simply as follows:

1st census	603,550
Plus 3000 who were slain before 1st census	3,000
Total =	606,550
Minus 24,000, 250 and 14,700 who died	38,950
Minus 14 others as already outlined above	14
Total =	567,586

The result of 567,586 proved to be almost the equivalent of 131 orbits of Jupiter at 567,569 days. There was 17 days of a short-fall.. The research was full of surprises for 567,586 as days proved to be 1,554 years or 777 + 777 solar years to the exact day. That result displayed the relationship between twice the periods of 777 temple years being in harmony with 131 orbits of the largest planet Jupiter. That royal planet with its divine relationship to twice the period of 777 temple years had also succumbed to those earthly numbers.

Just as with Saturn, a simulation exercise was carried out to establish the particular years when Jupiter would be closest in harmony with multiples of the solar years up to the period of 1,650 years. The results were that Jupiter intersected with multiple of the solar year after 261, 344, 605, 688, 949, 1,032, 1,293 and 1,376 years. There were six of those eight targets that could be formed from combinations of the numbers of each tribe in the Messiah time-frame. However, four of those results had a margin of error that was not truly in accord with harmonising the orbits of Jupiter to the solar year. But, the periods of 1,293 and 1,376 involved two pertinent line-ups of the tribes in the Messiah time-frame. The first line-up was as follows:

**Reuben + Simeon + Gad + Judah + Issachar
+ Zebulun + Ephraim + Dan + Naphtali = 472,240**

The total of the nine tribes at 472,240 as days was 18 days less than 1,293 years and also the equivalent of 12 days less than 109 orbits of Jupiter.

The second line-up with ten tribes was as follows:

**Reuben + Simeon + Gad + Judah + Issachar + Zebulun
+ Manasseh + Benjamin + Asher + Naphtali = 502,590**

That total of 502,590 as days was 17 days more than 1,376 years and was also 10 days more than 116 orbits of Jupiter at 502,580 days.

It would seem therefore, that it was the lengthy periods in time with 1,554, 1,376 and 1,293 years that the scribes engineered in the numerical archive. But why had they not factored in those lesser periods such as 344, 605 or 688 years as examples of the orbits of Jupiter being in harmony with multiples of the solar year? Perhaps, those lengthy periods were laying down a marker for further findings that will soon emerge with regard to the Star of Bethlehem. It was the period of 1,032 years that led to that opinion for it was also 87 orbits of Jupiter to within 5.6 leap days. The scribes had arranged a mini-grouping with the numbers between the names of Gad and Asher in the Messiah timeframe. Those numbers in that mini-group added up to 376,850, which was the equivalent of 1,031.78 years. The period of 1,031 years had been outlined previously as being 35 orbits of Saturn so the 1,031.78 years was nine months removed from that period. That nine month period would soon feature in an analysis involving Saturn and Jupiter together and it was felt that the scribes had factored in that period with the numbers to prepare the way for the star of Bethlehem.

The orbit of Jupiter is 50 days less than twelve solar years and that may be where the harmonisation with that planet and the solar year may have been catered for in the Bible. It outlined in the Book of Leviticus that the period of fifty days was to be measured out from the first Sabbath after the First-fruits accounting for seven Sabbaths plus an extra day. Note 18 Therefore, by building that period into their festivals it would have automatically harmonised the orbit of Jupiter with the solar year every twelve years. That period of an extra 50 days would apply just once every 12 years. The twelve tribes have often been associated with the twelve signs of the Zodiac but why not with the planet that had such a regal influence. It is possible that the story of the twelve year old Jesus getting lost in the temple for three days was a pointer in that direction. The Hebrew solar year was so accurate that they knew to add a leap day every four years. But, because the period of three days is so common in the Bible they may have corrected the leap day anomaly every twelve years by adding three extra days at the time of the Passover. Likewise, the correction of the 50 day anomaly with Jupiter may have been catered for at the next big festivity of the First-fruits.

THE STAR OF BETHLEHEM

Having established the importance of Saturn and Jupiter in the grand sweep of biblical history the investigation turned to examine if a conjunction of those two planets was perhaps what caused the Star of Bethlehem. Many scientific sources stated that the phenomena could have been a spectacular triple conjunction of those two planets in 7 BCE or a massing of Saturn, Jupiter and Mars in 6 BCE. The massing of those three planets occurs every 794.4 years. Note 19 Travelling back in time along the pathway of Luke's genealogy, the previous massing of those planets would have been in the year 801 BCE approx. and before that in 1,596 BCE. That time period of 1,596 BCE relative to Luke's genealogy would have been when the twins Esau and Jacob were born. There was a feeling of *DeJa Vu* about that finding as if the twins together in the womb were the metaphorical representation here on earth of those two heavenly bodies massing together. That image was not without foundation for there was a quote by Balaam in the Book of Numbers as follows:

"A star will come out of Jacob a sceptre will rise out of Israel... A ruler will come out of Jacob." Number's 24: 17.19

That statement had bothered scholars for centuries though now it was like a lighthouse steering the way to the Messiah. The massing of Jupiter and Saturn appears to have been the spectacular phenomenon. That can be ascertained by measuring out both those orbits starting at a common point in time from the year 1,596 BCE. The period started with the twins Esau and Jacob and ended at the births of John and Jesus as follows:

1,590 years = 580,735 days

Jupiter by 134 orbits = 580,567 days Shortfall of 5 ½ months to reach 1,590 years

Saturn by 54 orbits = 580,997 days Over-run of 9 months beyond 1,590 years

The picture that had materialised had some striking overtones when superimposed on the episodes of Elizabeth and Mary getting pregnant and delivering their two respective sons.

Elizabeth got pregnant and hid herself for 5 months. Mary got pregnant in the 6th month and went to visit her cousin Elizabeth. The two babies jumped in their wombs as if they were being reconciled. In contrast, Esau and Jacob had stirred in their mother Rebecca's stomach 1,590 years previously and God told her that there were two nations in her womb. Mary made a long salutation to Elizabeth and referred back to Abraham thus making a very notable linkage between the two periods. She stayed with Elizabeth for three months and then went home. Six months later Jesus was born. Contrast those events with the heavenly planetary movements on high as follows:

- Elizabeth got pregnant by divine intervention from on high and hid for 5 months while 134 orbits of the regal planet Jupiter was 5 ½ months of a shortfall from the period of 1,590 years

- Mary got pregnant in the 6th month which would be at the end of the 1,590 year period relative to the massing of the two planets.

- Mary visited Elizabeth and stayed for 3 months which compared with the same period as her forerunner called

Tamar who would soon prove to be the saviour of the sacred genealogy. Tamar was 3 months pregnant when Judah belatedly said that "she has been more righteous than I." Her story will be outlined later.

- Mary was pregnant for 9 months and the saviour Jesus was born while the 54 orbits of Saturn (the saviour of Israel) were 9 months longer than 1,590 years. Therefore, the two contrasting periods of nine months of Jesus in the womb and the orbit of Saturn would have run exactly in parallel with each other.

The outcome was as spectacular as any conjunction and there was sufficient evidence to state that the Star of Bethlehem had proved to be the massing of Jupiter and Saturn which began in 6 BCE. That heavenly scene continued into 5 BCE. Allowing for the overrun of nine months of Saturn and its parallel with Mary's pregnancy the birth of Jesus could be pinpointed to 5 or 4 BCE. Note 20

It was outlined in the last chapter about the difference of nine months between the 1,031 years with its 35 orbits of Saturn and the period of 1,031.78 years as derived from the listing of seven tribes in series. The totals of those seven tribes were just three months short of 87 orbits of Jupiter. The story of Elizabeth and Mary inferred three and nine month periods and the episode with Saturn and Jupiter as outlined also contained those two periods suggesting that they were pre-arranged to do so.

THE SEVENTH BIBLICAL TIME PERIOD OF 777 TEMPLE YEARS

The enormity of this discovery lies in the fact that it has revealed for the first time how a sacred timeline was laid down using red letter dates within which a pantheon of biblical superstars were introduced. The choreography and timing of each new arrival was prepared with the same painstaking effort used today to build up the profiles of celebrity VIPs. In contemporary parlance, the scribes took on the role of promoters. It has emerged in the course of these pages that the coming of the Messiah was the biggest PR undertaking in the history of mankind. Nothing was left to chance. The epiphany was preordained and plotted with systematic brilliance using mathematical wizardry. Provision was made by a golden circle to cast the stage production back in time to begin with the father figure Abraham. Each retrospective link was superimposed on previous history.

Looking to the future, the time line was predicted in advance for history to be overwritten upon. Day by day, the counting of time took place till the goal was in sight with the arrival of Jesus. Some 55 generations would eventually complete the family tree rooted in the work of those who devised the calendar of the gods.

For the first time, the Bible can be removed from the realms of faith and presented in more realistic language. The central thesis was that the coming of the Messiah was pre-ordained by painstaking forward planning to proclaim the sacred time line of the Lord. The truth was not, alas heralded by trumpeting angels, but lay on the very parchment of the Bible. That alternative story was not one of serpents and saints, but relied on hard facts based on detailed mathematical analysis. Simply put, all the milestones

The Mount of Olives

laid along the path for the Redeemer were prefabricated to authenticate his arrival at the end of days. The epiphany was prepared with methodical mastery by the Magi or by an elite initiate. Behind the scenes they employed a secret calendar of almost impossible intricacy which gave them the power of determination. The heavens were their dominion and they had the ability to forecast with total accuracy the unfolding of orchestrated mo mentous events. That power of the prophets was wielded through the calendar of the Gods.

Working on the basis that facts are sacred, this research has followed a series of mathematical sign posts laid down in the Book of Numbers and in other parts of the Bible. Those signpost clues led to the facts of the heavens, the realm of the gods. The ancients set down a pathway using the building blocks of numbers by which they could follow in the foot steps of God. From Jacob's ladder, the endeavour to scale the heavens if only in a dream, to the beguiling tower of Babel, the aspiration of mortal man was to soar up to the Almighty. Using their extraordinary understanding of math's the ancients constructed a bridge to infinity and thus achieved the divine attribute of immortality in the metaphorical sense. Their message was the most important ever communicated for it was no less than the word of God.

Step by step a cogent case emerged to suggest that by analysing in isolation the verbal content of the Bible, the message and significance of the numerical dimension was lost sight of. Up to now, cynics could immediately scoff: Was it credible that primitive goat herders and shepherds who relied upon the technology of the abacus to count their very flocks could actually compute on a par with Microsoft? But time has been the most tangent link between man and the heavens for millennia. Divine connections were made with the sun as day and the moon as night. Light and darkness, good and evil. That journey around the sun has had a sacred significance before the hourglass or sun-dial were ever devised.

The ingenuity of the calendar lay in the facts that it empowered the cogescenti. It was used to lay down a red carpet into a future along which a selection of Biblical heavyweights would eventually walk. Beginning with Abraham and then Isaac, the time-line moved on to introduce the dual personality of Jacob and Israel. The women involved were certainly exceptional in their relevance and projected role. Sarah, Rebecca and even Rachel, who became excluded from the Messiah time-frame, could not readily conceive. The overtures of a divine conception were sown with the intervention of God-Like interludes between Sarah, Rebecca and the almighty figures of Pharaoh and a King. There was also the relatively unknown character of Tamar who went beyond the realms of natural Hebrew expectation to ensure that the sacred Messiah genealogy was maintained. Then Jacob family numbering 70 persons in all moved to Egypt to be with Joseph.

A period of 430 years of silence would then pass before Moses would arrive on stage to manage the time line production with the counting of the days. The show continued with Joshua and many other rulers, or Judges, who fulfilled the historical role. A saintly figure called Samuel was ordained as the Lord's anointed and he selected Saul to be the first King of the Israelites. It was a disastrous choice. But Samuel's second attempt of choosing David to be king proved to be the centre stage of the Messiah time line with his two age periods of 30 and 40 years. David's reign was followed by his son Solomon who also reigned for 40 years and theirs was the golden age of the Israelite empire. After Solomon, the kingdom split apart and eventually descended into ruin. The most notable worthy characters along the historic highway were King Hezekiah and Josiah, Ezra and Nehemiah. In parallel with the historical enactment, there were almighty prophets such as Elijah, Isaiah, Jeremiah and a host of other forecasters. They were the forerunners who prepared the audience with the confluence of special indicators, signs or portents. Those signs were generally celestial and created a sense of divine connection. It imbued the character with a mystique or aura and culminated with the birth of Jesus Christ, and his receipt of the royal ointment from the Magi.

The temple calendar had opened up the windows of the Bible and at last the real time related predictions of a Messiah can be outlined. Some 55 generations would complete the family tree from Isaac to the arrival of Jesus at the end of days. He followed in the footsteps of the prophets and just like Solomon, he also rode through Jerusalem on a donkey. From Luke's and Mathew's genealogy it was established that the virtual biblical time period from the birth of Isaac to the birth of Jesus was 1,620 years. The attention then focused on measuring those lengthy periods with the temple calendar system. The pertinent period proved to be the time from the birth of Isaac to the death and resurrection of Jesus. That was a period of 55 times 30 years =1,650 years plus 3 years that Jesus was preaching. The total was 1,653 years or 603,745 ⅓ days. That period was measured out with the temple 777-day calendar and the result would explain why it stated at the crucifixion that the Messiah was numbered. The figures were as follows:

777 days by 777 times = 603,729 days -Target = 603,745 ⅓ days

The result of 777 days by 777 times was just 16 ⅓ days short of the period of 1,653 years that measured the time from the birth of Isaac to the resurrection of Jesus. That result was by any counts astounding for it was in fact 777 temple years.

The fundamental principle of having the temple calendar in harmonisation with the solar year was addressed with an end performance that would write that bridging leap day element into the minds of every generation to come. The biblical authors had chosen the ultimate sacred period of 777 temple years to be harmonised with 1,653 solar years. That shortfall of 16 ⅓ days was made up of the 14 day lead in to the most sacred period of Jewish worship, the Passover and with what was to become the most sacred period in Christian worship; the three days (almost) in the tomb.

The period of 1,653 years began with the birth of Isaac but the 777 temple years started at the end of the eight day when he was circumcised. It ended on the day when Jesus rode into Jerusalem in triumph, which was eight days before the resurrection. That was the end of days of that divine period of 777 temple years to the very day. In contrast, the parallel period of 1,653 years began with the birth of Isaac and ended on the day of Jesus resurrection.

After Jesus rode into Jerusalem he overturned the tables in the temple courtyard and released the doves. The numbers of the divine time line had been completed at the end of days so the image of the upturned tables in the temple was making an expressive statement. Jesus was pointing a finger at the table (pun for mathematical tables) that the Ark of the Covenant rested on and the dimensions of Solomon's temple where it was eventually housed. Those dimensions had the same numerical values and ratios in cubits as the three main time periods had in years and leap days as follows: Note 21

	Solomon's Temple In Cubits	Ark Table Cubits		Genealogy Periods Years	Leap Days
Courtyard Length	40	2	Matt	40	2
Height	30	1 ½	Luke	30	1 ½
Breadth	20	1	777	20	1

Via Dolorosa

The three measurements of the temple with the width, height and the length of courtyard (where Jesus upturned the tables) were all in direct ratio with the width, height and length of the table. And all three measurements of both the temple and the table were the equivalent to the three principal periods of 30, 20 and 40 years of the temple calendar together with their leap days. Those same three numbers of 20, 30 and 40 had been signalled at the beginning of the Messiah time-frame when Jacob presented his avenging brother Esau with animals to appease him. The present of those numbers of animals had proved to be of greater value to Esau than his birthright and fathers blessing, which Jacob had deviously acquired. Rather than attack Jacob, Esau embraced him with peace and love. Ironically, those two scenes with Esau and later with Jesus were confrontational and both faced up to the numbers of the temple calendar.

Esau had expressed love and peace and Jesus followed suit when the doves were set free. The dove is the symbol of peace so that act by Jesus would appear to be another pointed finger, which was most likely aimed at Chapter 7 of the Book of Numbers. In that chapter, each of the leaders of the twelve Tribes made a collection of offerings before Moses. One of those was the Peace Offering. That offering comprised of two oxen, five rams, five male goats and five male lambs to be sacrificed. When that Peace offering was presented in tabular format the result was as follows:

Oxen	Rams	Goats	Lambs
2	5	5	5

In that tabular format the number 2,555 became evident. The number 2,555 as days proved to be seven years of 365 days. Therefore, a new numerical format was evident and the notational value of the arrangement with those animals was now in units, tens, hundreds and thousands. Seven years was the sacred Sabbath period of the Hebrew's and it had been revealed as the secret numbers of the Peace Offering. That seven year period was well highlighted with Jacob having to wait two periods of seven years to marry his truelove Rachel and with Joseph forecasting seven years of plenty and seven years of famine. The cock crew and the three times were completed so this part of the story must end and fittingly, it finishes with Jesus and the symbol of peace. Shalom

Swords into Plough-Share, Isaiah

Summary

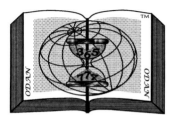

The greatest worldwide celebrations in history took place with the year 2,000 bi-millennium and that AD event actually stood as a testimony to the birth date of Jesus even if that fact was lost on many. That is a measure of the impact on time that the founding biblical fathers achieved with the launch of their Messiah. They had succeeded and achieved the impossible from a tiny patch of arid land called Israel so long ago. The Y2K revellers on that almighty day were the benefactors of an arcane philosophy based on love, peace and forgiveness. That philosophy laid the groundwork for the three revolutionary demands of equality, fraternity and justice that underpins our modern democracy. The predictions of those founding fathers were delivered on the crest of that great dominion of time.

One can only gaze in awe at the marvellous ingenuity of the creators to comprehend time itself. All through the findings the principle of Jewish economy was borne out in the patterns where the numbers were woven two by two as witnesses to a dualistic combat between orbital and linear time. That capability to make the calendar features conform to seven times with seven checksums in seven offerings throughout the encoding was a miraculous feat that would have required phenomenal levels of concentration, prodigious talent and painstaking skill. Its time dimension contents created perhaps the greatest enigma ever, one that would exhaust the limits of human investigative powers throughout history. There are no conspiracy theories with regard to this great wisdom having been concealed from the public. Rather, it is so obvious that the main churches did not inherit the encryption keys to that kingdom of the heavens. On faith alone they worshipped, not understanding the true symbolic meaning of the bread and wine relative to the body and blood of the sacrificial beasts. Such was the influence and mystique of that dominion the creators had bound within the Bible. People believed in it unaware that the facts and figures to master time were right before their eyes. That great saga of time so ingeniously concealed within the parables and narratives of religious history became the world's greatest bestseller. It was quite a triumph for its authors who lived thousands of years ago.

To demonstrate the enormous scope of those seven time lines it was necessary to rearrange them into a presentation to show where the relevant cosmic cycles of the planets provided a supporting measurement for the numerical periods.

1st and 2nd Time line: Luke's Genealogy and the Orbit of Saturn in parallel

- 30 years with 55 generations from Luke's Gospel = 1,650 years or 602,649 days

- The Messiah time-frame in the half-totals of the tribes was 602,640 days. The nine day shortfall proved to be deliberately factored in to allow for the circumcision on the eight day and thus provide the starting date for the 777 temple years.

- Running in parallel was 56 orbits of 29 years 198 days of Saturn = 602,515 days. Those 56 orbits of Saturn were bridged to the Messiah time table of 602,640 days where the scribes factored in 250 men to be swallowed up thus creating the required number of man-days lost. To reinforce the inclusion of the orbit of Saturn, the unique periods of 324, 707 and 1,031 years relative to those orbits being in harmony with the solar year were found recorded in the two censuses that were proven to represent days.

3rd and 4th Time line: Mathew's Genealogy and the Orbit of Venus in parallel

- 40 years with 42 generations from Mathew's Gospel = 1,680 years, which was the time span from Abraham to Jesus. That was the same result as with 56 generation of 30 years = 1,680 years with Luke's Gospel.

- The 40 year cycle of Venus (almost) at 14,605.5 days ran in parallel with Mathew's genealogy with 32 laps being revealed from the totals of nine tribes in sequence. The shortfall of 134 leap days to harmonise with 1,280 solar years was again provided from the outcome of the 250 who were consumed. But, like with Saturn, there was a nine day shortfall from total harmonisation with the solar year and that shortfall also proved to be deliberate.

- To reinforce the position the numbers of Leah's sons in the first census totalled 292,200 or 800 years, which was associated with the synodic cycle of Venus and made up half the Messiah time-frame. It was also the approximate period when the massing of Jupiter and Saturn occurred. i.e. every 795 years.

5th Time line with Jupiter

- In the 1st census where the 603,550 were totalled together with the man-days of about 3,000 and revealed the equivalent of 140 orbits of Jupiter. Then the 24,000, 14,700, 250 and 14 as man-days lost were subtracted and the result was the equivalent of 131 orbits of Jupiter in 1,554 years. The period of 1,554 years was twice 777 temple years.

- That initial result was reinforced by the findings from the Messiah time-frame. The first such finding was with the period of 1,293 years with its inherent 109 orbits of Jupiter. There was also the period of 1,376 years with its 116 orbits of Jupiter.

The Star of Bethlehem

The massing of Jupiter and Saturn every 795 years complimented the two previous outlines of the importance of Saturn and Jupiter in the cosmic measurement of time. The periods of approximately 5 months with Jupiter to harmonise with the solar year in 7 BCE followed by the 9 months overspill by Saturn were mirrored on the earth below with the conception of John, then Jesus from 'on high.' That was where Elizabeth was hiding for 5 months and the nine months that Mary was pregnant until her baby was born.

6ᵗʰ Time line: From Solomon to Jesus

The period from Solomon being crowned king the morning after David died to where the 30 year old Jesus began to preach was 1,000 years. It was measured with the temple 777 day year and its 52 leap days were factored into the measurement with the time Nehemiah took to build the 1,000 cubits long walls of Jerusalem.

- The days of 1,000 years were found archived in sequence as a part of the Messiah time-frame as the number 365,240. That effectively divided the time-frame in to two parts and the 476 years that was factored into the statement about Solomon building the temple was evident in that pre-temple part.

7TH Time line The Time Period of 777 Temple Years: The Messiah Time Line

- The 7th time line was with 777 Temple years of 603,729 days. That time line was harmonised with 1,653 years by the addition of the 14th day of the month to the Passover and the 3 days of Jesus in the tomb.

It seems incredible that such technical specifications of time were recorded secretly in the Bible. Many questions immediately arise such as, where did the Israelites acquire such a vast wisdom of time and how were their measurements so accurate? The results in these findings were achieved using modern arithmetic but yet, the ancients seemingly reached the same outcomes by whatever particular methods. Typecast images are of devout holy priests and prophets praying, fasting and meditating. These findings go many a step further to reveal that the ancients were immersed in astronomy and the art of mastering time. All those references to the watchers in the Bible have to be revisited for it may yield the observation posts with their 'high places' that were used by a 'stiff-necked' people. It is likely that the temple was the sanctuary where the gifted ones spent their years evaluating new numerical puzzles and arrangements to create the intelligent design that has just been revealed. Somewhere, there had to be an instruction manual to explain the structural layout of the great chessboard of eternal time?

That Messiah time line laid down a crimson trail through history written in blood, which as any forensic scientist will attest, has proven to be an indelible ink. It began with the near sacrifice of Isaac but the unlucky ram got caught instead. A red thread was added to the bloodline when Tamar was delivering her twins. Then the blood spilled over with the events surrounding the Passover where all the innocent first born children were slain. There was gruesome blood curdling scenes in the Book of Joshua where so many were slain by the sword. The image of the arrow hitting Josiah created its own target of a blood red full stop; providing a critical midway intermission in the historical time line saga. Right throughout the Messiah saga the divine ink supply was used to delineate the rituals of the burnt offerings. There would have been so much sacrificial blood spilt over the temple years and perhaps that was the reason why it came out of the winepress to the length of 1,600 furlongs. That number steeped in blood verified the days as having retained their original values.

At the early stages of the saga Judah did not want blood on his hands and suggested to his brothers that they should sell Joseph to passing traders. Joseph was sold for twenty pieces of silver and ended up in Egypt. Thus, because of Judah's suggestion, Joseph was saved from the pit that would have become his grave. At the end of the story Judas allegedly betrayed Jesus for thirty pieces of silver. The findings would suggest that Judas drew the shortest straw and gave the willing Jesus away like a bride at a wedding ceremony. Was Jesus, like Joseph, also to be saved? The reprieve of Isaac, who was the first in the Messiah timeline from being a human burnt offering, would imply that the same position would apply to the last in the chain. Indeed, Jesus even raised that situation when he chided the Pharisees that Abraham did not kill anyone so why should they want to kill him. Note 22

In the temple, Jesus read from the Book of Isaiah and perhaps that choice acknowledged the true source of the Gospels and the likely disseminator of the ancient wisdom. The time was on hand. There was animosity, betrayal, torture and incited humiliation throughout his passion. At his trial, he held a staff, which was unusual for a prisoner to have as it could be construed to be a weapon. But the staff had featured so prominently in the epic journey and appeared to have been carried like a baton by all his predecessors in the two genealogies. It was the end of days and the mission in time was accomplished, for the seeds of a new everlasting philosophy had been miraculously sown. Isaiah had laid the groundwork by stating that the blood and wine of the burnt offerings could not prevail forever and he outlined the essential requirements of a new creed. Jacob had depicted the sign of the cross when his two arms crossed over Ephraim and Manasseh to bless them. Beneath the crossover of his two grandsons names in the censuses lay the solar key to the hidden archive of time. Jesus concluded the Messiah bloodline epic with the image of his outstretched arms displayed as an enduring divine symbol for all time.

It may appear from those initial findings with the Messiah time line that a shroud has been placed on the divine like character of Jesus and the legitimacy of the resurrection. From the evidence outlined it would be easy to rush to such a judgement. Whoever he was, Jesus knew the final part of the plot and succumbed to its historical inevitability. He was born of the chosen people and he himself must have been particularly chosen, though not necessarily from birth. It is more likely that he was enlisted as a true follower that rose through the highest orders and acquired the ultimate conferral in the ancient wisdom of the elite brotherhood. But why would a sane rational individual be willing to go like a lamb to the slaughter unless, somehow, there was light at the end of three short days? Despite the enormity of these findings, that light remains a mystery for all we have to go on is how time was measured. But the knowledge gleaned from the findings does constitute a powerful exhibit when placed in context and provides ample scope for a historical revision of that momentous event. We do not know what depths of concentration those holy people were able to achieve when mediating or did time really matter in that trance-like state? From the recently discovered Gospel of Judas it can be discerned that Jesus wanted to transcend time but was restricted by the burden of his physical body. Isaiah had turned back the clock to allow King Hezekiah live another fifteen years while Elijah had departed to the heavens in a fiery chariot. The star of temple time could therefore expect some miraculous intervention. It was called the resurrection.

Throughout these findings there have always been at least two witnesses to testify a result as factual. The Catholic Church requires two proven miraculous cures before conferring sainthood. After the resurrection Jesus spoke to Mary Magdalene, conferred with two disciples and visited the eleven apostles. But strangely, no one recognised him as Jesus. He enticed the apostles to view his wounds and rebuked them because they did not believe it was him that had resurrected from the dead. But only one person declared that he would not believe it was Jesus unless he placed his hands into the wounds. The Gospels do not say that Thomas carried out the clinical test but he was the only one that demanded such forensic type proof. Something was severely amiss with that biblical authentication for there was thus only one true witness, doubting Thomas. In affect, the whole position of definable proof was turned on its head and doubting Thomas has become the common catch-phrase for presenting cast iron evidence. Thus, on the word of one man rested the pillars of Christian faith with the belief in the resurrection.

The mystery continued for the void left by Jesus was bridged with the sudden appearance on the scene of an unusual replacement named Saul. It was all too convenient that a person un-known in the Gospels just sprung out of nowhere, had a miracu-lous conversion, was instantly filled with profound understanding of the new philosophy and immediately took the helm. Just like so many of the repeat performances in the Bible, that linkage between Jesus and Saul seemed to be well prepared. The fore-runner was Jacob who was on his way from Syria when he had a wrestling match with the Lord and was re-named Israel. His eyes were opened, so much so, that he could declare to his brother Esau that seeing him was like seeing God. The outcome of the wrestling match resulted with Jacob's offspring becoming the in-fluential tribes of Israel that prepared the way for the Messiah on the desert highway. Jacob was on his way from Syria while Saul was on his way to Syria. Saul also had his name changed by the Lord who re-named him Paul and he regained his sight with far reaching consequences. The preaching's and letters of Paul be-came the inspired philosophy of Christianity where a risen Christ replaced the Jewish crucified Jesus. Note 23

But what of the eventual aspirations of a down trodden peo-ple? Could their plight have been envisaged as any worse than the exile to Babylon? The Jews had been prepared for the arrival of a Messiah and envisaged such a divine delivery as another David or Solomon. Those were the two enlightened kings who presided over their greatest empire. Jesus preached the message of love and peace but that philosophy would have been very suspect, particularly with the belligerent might of Rome in domination. Did it require the mob to be incited so as to implement the as-pirations of the original biblical architects? That poses a new im-ponderable of how those planners got their forecasts so accurate. i.e. not a limb shall be broken. Despite the best plans something was bound to go wrong and the outcome could never be expected to match up exactly with the forecasted clues. Clues, however ambiguous they might seem, were yet relative enough to verify to millions of Christians that Jesus was the Messiah. The temple calendar proves that Jesus was in the right place at the right time with the right CV to claim that title. The facts therefore assert that he is the indisputable Messiah of both Jew and Christian alike. What of those founding patriarchs? Did they ever envisage the unintended consequences because of their pre-planned necessity to include torture and martyrdom for their Messiah? In its wake, the Jews would face persecution and almost extermination during the following nineteen hundred years. In recent times, centuries of cultural vilification has been addressed. But these findings reveal that the Jews were themselves the innocent party for the real plot was written in blood to be stigmatised in blood.

Note 24

PART II

CHAPTER 6

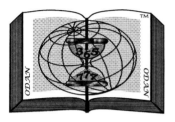

THE DRESS REHEARSAL IN THE DESERT

The Bible is itself a kind of miracle: The first great global communications project. Its reach could hardly be rivaled even today in the age of cable, satellite and 24 hour broadcasting. Its fascination has held millions enthralled through the centuries. Its gravity has reshaped borders, created dynasties and toppled kings. The writings of the standing armies of scholars who have pored over its every word could wallpaper the heavens. In the context of such exhaustive scrutiny, it must appear incredible that something so momentous could have been over-looked. Not since Samson flexed the full span of his mighty arms to bring the temple crashing down, have the pillars of conventional belief been so sorely tested. That scene with Samson appears to have been intended for in one fell swoop the house of cards came crumbling down to finally display the pillars of the temple calendar. There were so many revelations in the foregoing pages that may have made the findings overwhelming, particularly where some of the mathematical computations required keen levels of concentration. But the seals of the book within a book were finally broken and the higher mysterious language of the prophets can at last be understood.

That higher language employed the extremes of human senses to perceive what lay mysteriously behind natural terms such as 'digging wells' or sitting beneath an oak tree. The inner meanings transcend time and space and in reality it was like speaking one universal language. For instance digging wells implied the action of divining them first while an oak tree had the added dimension of being the earthly representative of the planet Jupiter. In turn Jupiter had a regal image of influencing the anointing of kings. Those were the keys to understanding the written words and the evidence led to the realisation that the journey to the Promised Land of milk and honey may have had a very different intended destination. That alternative metaphorical path may have led instead to the afterlife in the Milky Way that the Egyptians aspired to. For the first time in thousands of years it is now possible to learn to read that ancient story as the scribes intended in the higher interactive language.

ABRAHAM AND SARAH

The story began on a hot day with the desert air forming a haze on the horizon a man called Abram sat beneath the big oak trees at the camp where he lived in a place called Marme. He had come from afar with his wife Sarai and they had wandered with their herds and flocks seeking a fair land of plenty to settle. Those were nomadic times when the grazing and watering demands of animals determined the route while the owners often followed that course acceptingly. The warm winds from the desert were calmly blowing from the hazy hue on the dusty horizon. Out of that haze from the mists of time three strangers trudged forth making their way to the sprawling encampment. Abram had observed them in the distance and, on realising that they were directly coming his way, he rose up to greet them. The strangers were made very welcome by Abram and hospitality to dine as honoured guests was duly organised. Images of the prodigal son sprung to mind for Abram selected and prepared the tender calf for the celebration. It was to become one of the strangest encounters in the history of the Hebrews.

The three men were on a mission and they soon set out their plans. In what appeared to be a very far fetched statement they predicted that Sarai would bear a son even though she was ninety years old. From that offspring Abram would be the father of a dynasty that would be as numerous as the stars in the heavens. It was such an incredible prediction to make, so much so that the eavesdropping Sarai laughed in disbelief. The story then took a twist when God intervened to chastise Sarai for laughing but she denied doing so. God had previously spoken to Abram and had also promised that Sarai would conceive a bear him a son. The main difference in the two encounters was that on the first occasion, God made a covenant with Abraham that all males in his family were to be circumcised. Abram was then renamed Abraham while Sarai was renamed Sarah meaning princess. Even at that early stage of the story the composition was full of natures' language such as an oak tree contains rings within its trunk that represents each year of growth while in contrast, Abraham was being promised the lineage of a family tree.

The three men then depart promising that they would return at that time of life. There was no sign of them making that second coming in the Old Testament but two of them did arrive at Sodom and Gomorrah. The other one took on the profile of the Lord and waited around while Abraham pleaded with him to save the inhabitants of the two doomed cities. The Biblical story then outlined the events at Sodom and Gomorrah so it was necessary to deviate on that course to see why the scribes created that diversion.

The two holy men arrived in Sodom and stayed with Abram's nephew Lot. Soon the Sodomites came in force to take sexual advantage of the two holy men. In defence, Lot offered them his two daughters who have never 'known' men but the Sodomites had no interest in women. With the help of God the sodomites were blinded and could not find their way. Because of the pending disaster the two men from God pleaded with Lot and his family to leave. But, it would appear that Lot and his family were also gay and lesbian for they had to be led by the hand to safety thus inferring that they were also blinded. The lord poured fire and brimstone on Sodom and Gomorrah and the two cities were destroyed. Lot and his family were told not to look back but in the heat of the moment, Lot's wife disobeyed and was turned into a pillar of salt for looking back.

The purpose of that story of Sodom and Gomorrah appeared to be 'ring out the old, ring in the new.' The new beginning was where Abraham and Sarah had the promise of a son whose descendants would be as numerous as the stars of the heavens. In contrast the first episode of the Bible with the stories of Adam and Noah and the numbers of their descendants were being consigned to history. The theme of the story was not to look back. In that regard the Sodomites were blinded and could not see at all. But seemingly, so were Lot and his family as they had to be led by the hand. Therefore, it was surprising that Lot's wife was turned into a pillar of salt for allegedly looking back seeing that she appeared to have been already blinded. By association, the pillar of salt brought to mind the pillars of wisdom that were obviously being put into cold storage. Those two pillars were referred to by Josephus as having been handed down from before the flood and which contained the statistics of the heavens. To verify the view that the pillars were being put into cold storage it was no coincidence that salt was prescribed for it is a preservative. Therefore, it would appear that the scribes were conveying to us in the higher meaning not to look back at the pillars that were being covered up and left behind. Is it beyond coincidence that the greatest pillars in the biblical lands, the pyramids, were initially coated in white limestone to preserve them and were in that condition until the 6th century CE? The whole theme was not to look back and the scribes used all the resources at their disposal to get the message across. They even resorted to utilise that concept in the backside act of sodomy to force home the issue.

The first sexual scene in the Bible was with Adam and Eve and it has dominated the headlines as if it were the only promiscuous act in the whole book. Yet, Adam and Eve were consenting adults who were only doing what nature intended at a time when there was no formal institution of marriage to restrict their desires. In contrast, the Messiah storyline involved several uncensored acts with extra-marital sexual encounters that were out of character with the religious theme of the Bible. For instance, when Lots two daughters thought that there were no men left in the world they turned to their father for intercourse. They got him drunk on wine on two successive nights and then enticed him to have sex with them. He obliged, but because of the wine he had a memory lapse of the events. So a final message of forgetfulness was deployed by the scribes suggesting that the pillars of wisdom were purged from human memory. Thus the new story could begin bringing the contents of those two pillars to life. Therefore, it was time to move on to Abraham and Sarah and follow their family tree.

The extra marital encounters continued where Abraham and Sarah went down to Egypt at the time of a famine. It appeared that hunger would drive a man to any limits for Abraham passed off his wife as his sister to the Egyptians just in case he should be harmed by envious admirers of her beauty. But it was the highest lord of all with the mighty Pharaoh who was captivated by Sarah's beauty and he slept with her. Pharaohs were adored as Gods so this interlude created a divine image of 'on high.' In due course there was another famine and this time Abraham passed off Sarah as his sister to a King named Abimelech who willingly took her. The contradiction in the story with Pharaoh and King Abimelech was that Sarah was supposed to be an old barren woman of ninety years old.

The possibility of the outcome of those two encounters was that Pharaoh, King Abimelech or Abraham could have been the father of Isaac. The first two with Pharaoh and a king were royalty and would be considered as gods while Abraham was Gods chosen mortal. It was relative for the name Sarah meant princess and Abimelech was a Semitic name meaning 'father of the king.' so the highness of royalty was openly implied. All the signs were that the promised son was to be supernaturally conceived and would form the beginning of a regal line. As the three men foretold, a son was born and he was named Isaac. But there was no mention of the three men from God returning to proclaim the event. Instead there was a ceremonial ritual on the eight day after the birth when the baby Isaac was circumcised. It is strange that the supernatural conception of Jesus by Mary from 'on high' is paramount to Christianity but the conception of Isaac by the aged barren Sarah with similar 'on high' undertones never gets a mention. But now that the two events are directly linked by 777 temple years of the Messiah time line, it reveals that the story was designed so that Isaac and Jesus were seen to be supernaturally conceived giving them the mantle of a divine birthright.

In the encounter with king Abimelech the episode of digging wells arose. Several wells were dug by Abraham and of course, the spring from which the water arose had first to be identified with the use of a divining rod. The king recognised that Abraham was favoured by God and asked him to show kindness to all his family. In turn, Abraham gave the king sheep and cattle and set aside seven ewe lambs in recognition that he (Abraham) had dug the well. So the place was called Beersheba because the two men made an oath there. Those seven ewe lambs that Abraham gave to the king were the first instalments of the burnt offerings. The starting point of the Messiah time-frame was clearly being identified with the divining rod of the two genealogies pointing to the spot. Earlier in the story the barren Sarah had encouraged Abraham to sleep with her Egyptian handmaid Hagar and a son called Ishmael had been born of that union. Now that Sarah had her own son Isaac she got Abraham to send Hagar and Ishmael away. Isaac grew up but in a test of faith with God, Abraham was prepared to make a blood sacrifice of his son in what would have been a human burnt offering. At the last minute, God restrained Abraham and an unlucky ram that was caught in a bush was offered up instead. (Isaac did not burn and many generations later Moses would encounter a burning bush that did not burn)

ISAAC AND REBECCA

When Isaac had grown to manhood his father arranged for his trusted servant to find a wife for his son from within his extended family far away at Ur. On arriving at Ur, the servant was greeted by a young woman called Rebecca who gladly watered the servant's camels. Something was gravely amiss however for at that stage of development historians are of the opinion that the camel had not been domesticated as a beast of burden. The marriage prearrangement took place with Abraham's servant offering Rebecca two gold bracelets and a nose ring. Eventually, Isaac married Rebecca who came to him riding on a camel.

In due course there was another famine in the land and Isaac and Rebecca headed for greener pastures at a place called Gerar. Isaac passed off his wife Rebecca as his sister to, of all people, King Abimelech. They stayed a long time and one day Abimelech saw Isaac caressing Rebecca and realised she was his wife. The episode with digging wells was also repeated for the Philistines fearing Isaac's growing wealth filled in the wells so that his stock could not be watered. Therefore, Isaac had to intervene with King Abimelech and would likely have had to divine for the springs again especially if the wells had been filled with desert sand. This time the divining rod of the two genealogies was pointing at the conception of Rebecca. She got pregnant with twins and when they jostled inside her she was told by God that two nations were in her womb. The implication of the episode with Abimelech was that Rebecca's twin sons Esau and Jacob could have been the offspring of the king or of Isaac? The encounter with a king again introduced those royal concepts such as the planet Jupiter being the sign of the anointing of kings or the regal stamp of being conceived from 'on high.'

JACOB AND ISRAEL

The twins were born with Esau first but Jacob held his heel. Because Esau was the first born he was heir apparent to his fathers blessing. However, when the two boys were grown into men Jacob outwitted the faint hungered Esau and acquired his older brother's birthright for what has become known as a mess of pottage. Later, Rebecca contrived with her favourite son Jacob and they deceived the dim sighted Isaac into giving the younger son his fathers blessing. There was something gravely amiss with the Biblical story for the old dim sighted Isaac allegedly lived for perhaps another 100 biblical years. Esau in retaliation to Jacob's deceit threatened to kill his devious brother but Rebecca sent the younger son off to her brother Laban in Syria. On his journey to Syria bearing a staff as his sole possession, Jacob fell asleep using a wayside stone for a pillow. Most pillows are made from feathers so the dream he was about to have turned out to be uplifting. Jacob dreamt he saw a ladder that reached to the heavens and there were angels ascending and descending on it. The notion of a bridge to the heavens was born with the ladder resting on the foundation stone or pillow, while the rungs would be numbered later in the census of the tribes of Israel. (Jacob was also named Israel) An abacus can be visualised with the rungs of that ladder.

Jacob arrived in Syria and met his first cousin Rachel who was watering her families flocks of sheep. Jacob had but a staff and the sheep were being watered prompting images of a divining rod. It was love at first sight and Jacob agreed to work seven years for his uncle Laban to procure Rachel's hand in marriage. Therefore, Jacob had to wait for the equivalent of the sabbatical period of seven years, which was a total of 2,555 days. Eventually the day arrived for the marriage of Jacob and Rachael. But Laban outwitted the wily Jacob in what has to be viewed as poetic justice. Laban sent in the older less attractive sister Leah into the bridal suite. (Biblical sources state that Leah and Rachel were also twins) Jacob was waiting eagerly in the dark and knew no difference. The episode had all the flair for a modern soap opera and one can only imagine the expression on Jacob's face on seeing Leah the next morning? He moaned to his uncle of having been short changed but Laban chided him about the custom of the oldest daughter having to be the first to be married. In reality, the wily Jacob got what he deserved for his devious treatment of his older brother. Laban drove a hard bargain and Jacob had to work another seven years of 2,555 days to finally marry his beloved Rachel.

The central numerical theme in the story was the period of seven years. In Chapter 7 of the Book of Numbers each of the leaders of the twelve Tribes of Israel made a collection of offerings before Moses. One of those was the Peace Offering. That offering comprised of two oxen, five rams, five male goats and five male lambs to be sacrificed. When that Peace offering was presented in tabular format the result was 2,555 or the equivalent of seven years of 365 days. Seven years was the sacred Sabbatical period of the Hebrews and it had been revealed as the secret numbers of the Peace Offering. That episode with Jacob involved two periods of seven years and later there would be two periods of seven years with Joseph interpreting Pharaoh's dream about the famine in Egypt.

In due course Leah gave birth to sons. Jacob had eventually married his beloved Rachel but she could not conceive and felt isolated and forlorn. The extra marital affairs continued where the two sisters gave their maid servants Zilpah and Bilah to Jacob and both delivered two sons each. Rachel acquired a 'mandrake' from her sister which had been brought home by Leah's oldest son Reuben. Because of the magical properties of this 'mandrake' it would seem that Rachel eventually conceived, thus continuing the theme of a supernatural birth. To her was born a son whom she named Joseph. He was destined to become Lord apparent over the mighty kingdom of Egypt.

Jacob worked for seven plus seven years and then another six years for his Uncle Laban making it a total of 20 years in all. That period of 20 years was a central part of the blueprint of the Temple calendar. i.e. one leap day to be added every 20 years. There were some intricate manipulations between Jacob and his uncle about acquiring ownership of all the new stock that was bred. But the devious Jacob got the upper hand by spiking the breeding habits of the herds and flocks and his share greatly increased while Laban's share grew inferior and diminished. At the end of those 20 years Jacob gathered up his wives, maidservants and family together with the stock he claimed ownership of and departed without Laban's knowledge. In that Exodus Rachel stole her father's images.

Laban was furious and pursued Jacob until they confronted

each other. But after the shouting match was over they made a covenant over a heap of stones and peace prevailed. On coming to Syria, Jacob's head had rested upon a stone and in his dream that stone was the foundation for his heavenly ladder. Twenty years later, on coming out of Syria with eleven sons and one about to be conceived, the heap of stones would appear to be the metaphorical steps for that stairway to the heavens. But there was still the matter of the stolen images and it would appear they were of major importance to Laban, or more aptly to the time related story. Laban searched for his images throughout the camp until he came to Rachel's tent. Rachel sat on the camel's harness beneath which she had hidden those images. She declared she could not move because of her period and so her menstrual cycle saved the day. The authors of this great biblical epic were making a covert statement when they introduced the menstrual cycle to hide images. Images were considered to be false Gods and lunar time was also a false period. The relationship of the lunar month with female periods was been drawn for both cycles are practically of similar lengths. It was also perhaps an insinuation that another supernatural pregnancy could be expected. Indeed, that appeared to have been Rachel's last period for the story continued where she becomes pregnant with her second child Benjamin. That indirect clue with the false god of the lunar cycle was a signpost prompt for it transpired that in the first census of the twelve tribes of Israel (Jacob) the numbers of Benjamin was 35,400, which is one hundred lunar years. Just as with the earlier example with Jacob and the seven years, the menstrual cycle of his wife Rachel was also giving a new insight into the secret planning layout of the Bible.

Jacob was returning home and on the way he had a wrestling match with the Lord. That wrestling match was a defining moment in Jewish history for on the morning after the Lord changed Jacob's name to Israel. On that day the concept of the Israelites was born. Jacob anticipated that he could expect trouble from his brother Esau because of his previous treatment of him. He divided his flocks in two lots and chose selected numbers to give to Esau, which in particular included 20 male goats, 20 rams, 30 female camels, 40 cows and 20 male donkeys. Jacob had selected those numbers specifically as a very special present to appease his brother. Although Esau was accompanied by four hundred men there was no battle. Instead Esau embraced his usurping brother in an act that was not unlike the philosophy of the Messiah, Jesus. i.e. Showing love and forgiveness. That outcome would suggest that the selected numbers of stock had to be of equal or more value than the older sons' birthright and the blessing of his father Isaac. That proved to be the case for the numbers of stock had the main values of numbers relative to the years that mapped the highway of the Messiah time line. After the encounter Jacob moved on and stopped at a place called Bethlehem where Rachel went into labour. She died giving birth to Jacob's twelfth son whom he named Benjamin. The link with Bethlehem would later lead to the prophet Jeremiah's quote in the Gospels about *"Rachel weeping for her children for they were not."*

JOSEPH

Those twelve sons of Jacob could mistakenly be considered to be the twelve tribes of Israel but that was not quite true for Levi and Joseph were omitted. Their positions were filled by Joseph's two sons Manasseh and Ephraim. Behind that replacement a deeper mystery lay hidden. Joseph was Jacob's favourite son and he seemingly possessed the ability to dream and interpret dreams and thus prophesise future events. Because of that favouritism and visionary abilities, Joseph was detested by his older

Sphinx and Pyramid

half brothers who were naturally all sons of the other mothers. The issue came to a head when Joseph told his family that he had a dream which showed the sun, moon and eleven stars bowing down to him. Jacob feared for Joseph and chided him for what he understood to be Joseph's father, mother and eleven brothers bowing down to him. There was an anomaly in the story for Joseph's mother Rachel was already dead. But the dream was a sign of things to come for Joseph would one day be in charge of the mighty kingdom of Egypt.

While tending to the family flock the brothers imprisoned the younger seventeen year old Joseph and practically buried him in a pit. (Shades of a grave) At his brother Judah's insistence that they should have no blood on their hands the brothers sold Joseph off to a caravan of passing traders for twenty pieces of silver. The traders were on their way to Egypt bearing spicery, balm and myrrh which they could expect to trade possibly for gold. Spicery, balm and myrrh and the expected payments in gold were also evident with Jesus. Joseph was sold as a servant to a nobleman called Potiphar. In due course, Potiphar's wife took a fancy to Joseph and she made strenuous advances to have promiscuous relations with him. Joseph was a power of virtue and feigned off all her advances.

In revenge, she pretended that Joseph tried to take advantage of her and produced the cloak she had snatched off him as evidence to prove her accusation. (Shades of the young man that was with Jesus at his arrest in the garden of Gethsemane who ran off naked when his linen cloak was snatched from him) Joseph ended up in jail for twelve years.

While in prison, Joseph interpreted the dreams of two inmates from Pharaoh's household. Years later, the mighty Pharaoh had two disturbing dreams which all his seers could not interpret for him. One of the former prisoners remembered Joseph with his visionary abilities and that led to him being brought out of prison and placed before Pharaoh. He interpreted the two dreams for Pharaoh, which forecasted seven year of famine. But first there would be seven years of plenty thus giving time to plan ahead and take remedial action. Pharaoh fully accepted the prisoners' word without question. Indeed, Pharaoh was so impressed that he made Joseph his second in command over what was the greatest dynasty and empire to have emerged at that time. Joseph took command and planned the next seven years of harvest and stored the abundant grain in storehouses. He had foretold that there would be seven years of famine throughout the lands of Egypt and the bad days duly arrived. Joseph held the keys of salvation and was able to provide food to the whole population to survive. In a twist of fate, his half brothers came to him from Canaan for assistance. After several interactive scenes Joseph forgave his deviant brothers and brought Jacob and his whole family to live in luxury where they got to occupy the best lands of Egypt.

If nothing else happened in the story commentators would have enough proof to declare that the promises and predictions made to Abraham had certainly come true. His great grand son Joseph was virtually in command of the powerful dynasty of Egypt. But there was a deeper story behind the façade for, despite Joseph having been the favourite son and having achieved second in command to Pharaoh, he did not feature in the two genealogies of the Messiah timeline. The oldest son Reuben also missed out for he slept with his father's maid servant. In what appears to be an insertion in the Book of Genesis the genealogy was passed onto Judah, but strangely through his son by his daughter-in- law Tamar.

TAMAR

Tamar is practically an unknown figure in the Bible yet she made an immense contribution in saving the Messiah genealogies. She struck a blow for women's liberation when she challenged the whole male prerogative of the Biblical patriarchs and won. Her story began just two generations after the twins Esau and Jacob and curiously it also involved twins. In what appears to be an insertion in the Book of Genesis Tamar married Judah's son Err. For bad behaviour, God slew Err. In line with Jewish custom Judah ensured that his next oldest son Onan married Tamar. Onan behaved with a 1960s liberated outlook to matchmaking and masturbated in contempt before Tamar. So God also slew him. It was then up to Judah to offer his youngest son Shelah to Tamar when he grew to adulthood. However, Judah hesitated in fear he would also lose his last son. When Shelah grew up Judah ignored his obligation to Tamar and eventually, when his wife died, he headed off to far away hills to shear sheep.

A determined Tamar shed her mourning clothes and dressed up in more attractive attire. She sat by the roadside and Judah on passing did not recognise her but believed her to be a harlot. He had no funds on him to pay her for the pleasure but promised her a young goat instead. However, Tamar asked as a pledge for Judah's staff, seal and cord (Also known as staff, signet ring and bracelet) and he willingly conceded them to her until he could deliver the goat to pay her. Tamar had thus achieved no less than the royal seal of the Messiah bloodline and it would appear to be on par with Jacob acquiring Esau's birthright and fathers blessing. Indeed, the only inheritance that Jacob carried with him on his way to Syria was a staff so it must have been the royal seal of office. Now, Jacob's son and heir Judah surrendered his regal staff and the emblems of his bloodline lineage to what he perceived to be a harlot. That was the same Judah who had sold his brother Joseph into Egypt for twenty pieces of silver so as not to have blood on his hands. In effect, Tamar had behaved nobly and saved the Messiah genealogies that seemed to have suddenly switched from Joseph to Judah. Those genealogies were shaped like a divining rod or staff so Tamar had acquired the royal inheritance with Judah's staff. When Judah returned with the young goat and could not find Tamar, he decided to let her keep those emblems least he became a subject of ridicule. It was noticeable that the staff, seal and cord appeared to be even more valuable than what Rebecca had earlier received as a potential bride for Isaac. The lineage between Rebecca and Tamar was therefore put on a natural heredity type footing and strangely, they both had twins

When Tamar was three months pregnant, Judah was told his daughter in law was pregnant and thus was declared a prostitute. In typical manly fashion he declared that she would be burned to death. In her defence, Tamar produced the staff, seal and cord to Judah and thus threw down the gauntlet to the whole Jewish male establishment. He had an immediate change of heart and solemnly declared *"that she is more righteous than I."* Those three months had a common theme many generations later with the pregnant Mary, for she visited Elizabeth and stayed for three months. Tamar's courageous act possibly insured that the unmarried Mary was not burned or stoned when she was found to be pregnant. Though Mary's pregnancy troubled him, her espoused husband named Joseph, whose father was noticeably named Jacob, had a dream that he was to protect her. The only other Joseph to have a dream was the son of the patriarch Jacob. Tamar had thus paved the way for Mary to conceive outside marriage with the most important infant in the Bible.

In due course Tamar delivered twin boys in what appeared to have similar tidings to the birth of Rebecca's twins. The first baby put out his hand and the midwife tied a red thread to it.

The hand was drawn back and the other baby was born first. He was called Perez. The actions by Tamar had thus saved the Messianic genealogies and she would appear to be the first women's libber in Biblical history. She had demonstrated that a woman could get pregnant with honour out of wedlock. Tamar's actions were accredited centuries later where another woman called Ruth had to intervene with her aging unmarried employer Boaz. Ruth lay at Boaz feet as he slept on the trashing floor. After Ruth's actions, Boaz sought general approval from the male establishment to marry her. They got married and she conceived and so Ruth thus saved the Messianic genealogies. When their son was born he was specifically listed as the descendant of Tamar and Perez. In turn Boaz became the great grandfather of David.

It would appear by her actions that Tamar was the very likely candidate for the missing name in Mathew's genealogy particularly as the omission was between Abraham to David. In that genealogy it stated that there were 42 generations from Abraham to Jesus but it only listed 41 names. The missing name was possibly between Abraham and David for the latter was listed twice. Tamar had the righteous credentials and was the holder of the staff, seal and cord of the Messiah bloodline. She was also the likely candidate to be the unnamed missing person in the riddle with 70 of Jacob's household who were with him on his arrival in Egypt as outlined in Chapter 46 of Genesis. All the names as listed when counted up came to 69 but the total listed was 70 and did not include Tamar. She had the emblems of the bloodline, was more righteous than Judah and was not a wife of any of Jacobs' sons or living grandsons. Therefore, Tamar would have fulfilled the criteria specified in Genesis. That is the end of the first episode of the stage production version of the Bible story and we are led to believe that 430 years would pass before the next character called Moses appeared on stage.

MOSES

Throughout the Old Testament there was no leader to compare with the awesome demanding figure of Moses. Abraham, Isaac and Jacob were mere adventurers compared with his role and stature. Abraham may have had a few words here and there with God and got his rewards in fathering Isaac in old age. Jacob had a wrestling match with the Lord, dreamt of an angel laden ladder and was allowed to conduct devious manipulations with his brother and uncle for his own gain. He was rewarded with becoming the father of the twelve tribes of Israel. But Moses was cast as the upright role model for the generations of the Hebrews. He spoke directly with God with neighbourly friendship and took copious notes on par with any private secretary. He faced down a mighty Pharaoh, parted the Red Sea and performed miraculous feats in times of dire need. Without his guidance and teaching skills, the twelve tribes of Israel would probably be no more than a forgotten band of nomads. Moses showed his mathematical abilities where he conducted the two censuses of the twelve tribes and then went a step further with a devised ratio system to divide the spoils of war by lots as shown in Chapter 31 of Numbers. He wrote the laws and introduced the sacred offerings to the Lord. His reward was to suffer the moans, groans, unfaithfulness and open rebellion of an ungrateful idolatrous group of ex-slaves that were privileged to be the chosen people. For their defiance, the original group of Israelites that escaped out of slavery in Egypt did not get to live long enough to see the Promised Land. Moses, for all his endurances went unrewarded and was destined not to set foot on that cherished land of milk and honey.

That was the stage portfolio of Moses but seemingly most of that story was contrived many centuries later by a priestly author called P. However, within his CV there was another profile of

Moses to be discerned. We are told that he was raised as an adopted son of Pharaoh's daughter and this privileged position would have afforded him direct access to the wisdom of the longest and most successful dynasty at that point in history. That Egyptian dynasty was already over three thousand years in existence at the time of Moses and the great Pyramids were then more than one thousand years old. The nearest comparison today with such a dynasty would be if he had been reared with the British Monarchy and had recourse to all its vast privileges. In that regard Moses would likely be a graduate of Cambridge or Oxford, possibly a patron of the Royal Astronomical society and have the vast British archives available to the monarchy as a library. Depending on the period, Moses could have discussed outer space theory with Hawkins or exchanged war tactics with Churchill. It is not far fetched therefore to suggest that in Egypt, Moses had recourse to study the original building plans of the great pyramids and held the royal rank to acquire the secret knowledge of the Egyptian priesthood.

It seems that Moses was allocated a role that would suggest he was the author of the first five books of the Bible. In that regard, it is more likely that Moses wrote out particular sections that included those lists of numbers and associated mathematical instructions. The Bible specifically states he carried two tables when coming down from the mountain after chiselling out the Ten Commandments. There was something amiss with that claim for tables are the medium for numbers and arithmetic and not for text. Surprisingly, the two tables of stone were lost in time but the scrolls appear to have been more robust and resilient. For instance, it outlines in the Book of Deuteronomy that just before his death Moses dictated or wrote out the law from beginning to end. If there was such a statesman who had a noble upbringing with privileged opportunities it was likely that he had a lot to write about. Those closest to him would surely have wanted to know of the great mysteries of the Egyptians, about their afterlife with the Gods in the Milky Way and if the Pyramids contained vast treasures. But knowledge acquired from positions of royalty or priesthood was sacred and could not to be disclosed to the masses under any circumstances. Perhaps that is the reason why the temple calendar was encoded secretly into the history of the Israelites that would later become the Bible.

THE DRESS REHEARSAL IN THE DESERT

The Messiah time line began with Abraham but the whole episode and events of the forty years in the wilderness was the miniature theatre to lay out the script. The setting was the desert of Sinai, the actors were the Israelites, the performance took forty years and the audience would be the universal eyes of millions. It had the numbers of days disguised as the two exaggerated censuses of the tribes that compassed the overall highway of 1,650 years. The orbits of those heavenly Gods of Jupiter, Saturn and Venus were captured beneath the steady gaze of those empowering numbers. There were forty two generations in Mathew's genealogy and each step was laid out in the moves and stops the Israelites made from Ramases in Egypt to the last pause before the entry into the Promised Land. In the higher language of symbolism and coded numerical formula, the blueprint of the temple calendar was woven into the rituals of the burnt offerings for the generations to come. The wandering Israelites would be embroiled in many squabbles with Moses who would appear to be divinely inspired in providing water from a rock and manna from the sky.

"Make Straight in the Desert a Highway for our God"

Isaiah 40:3

There were scenes of false idolatry, promiscuous relations with strange women and breach of the Sabbath day. Instrumental in all those side shows were specific numbers.

Those numbers were grafted into the story where for instance, particular numbers of people were killed by the plague or slaughtered on the command of Moses as a punishment for wrong doing. The real values of those numbers as time periods were revealed earlier with the orbits of Saturn, Jupiter, Venus and the solar year. The cast were condemned to wander in the desert for forty years travelling in a semi-circle rather than making a bee line for the Promised Land of milk and honey. Moses got the star role but the production would in time give profiles and personalities to many other chosen people who would become renowned camp side names through the generations.

After the Israelites had travelled a year and a month we are led to believe that Moses conducted a census of the twelve tribes of Israel. Each of the men of twenty years and upwards was counted by name. But with the census each man was also a number. In that way the men were chosen one by one and it states in the Book of Numbers that records had been kept to prove that they were the correct age. It was akin to producing a birth certificate. Even that part of the story about having such records seems far fetched seeing that the Israelites were supposed to have been slaves in Egypt. It was hardly the ideal setting to keep filing cabinets and a complement of office staff to enter the records. Those records would have been quite numerous for the total of the men of twenty years and upwards was given as 603,550 in number. Allowing for women, children, grandparents and grandchildren and others as stated in the Bible, the whole contingent would be in the region of two million people. That population would be the size of a major modern city and has already been compared to the city of New Orleans, which had a population of 1.4 million when hurricane Katrina struck. The Bible tells us that the Israelites got out so fast that they did not even get time to bake the bread but carried the knead on their shoulders. Yet, those hurried scenes were no obstacle for snapping up family records such as birth certificates.

There were two versions of the story running side by side for it also outlined that there were only four generations from Jacob to Moses and they were listed by name. It took Jacob with two wives and two maids twenty years to have twelve sons and one daughter. That was against a background where his grandmother Sarah was barren till old age, Rebecca took perhaps twenty years to get pregnant and Jacob's wife Rachel could not conceive for years. Jacob's whole family who went to Egypt including Joseph, Manasseh and Ephraim numbered seventy people. Therefore, there could not have been more than several hundred people after just four generations in Egypt, which proved that the number of 603,550 men was prefabricated. But to give credence to the total number of 603,550 men the historical time line was also prefabricated and the period of 430 years was introduced.

That period of 430 years had confused the whole natural time flow of Bible history. For instance, at the time of King Solomon it stated that the building of the temple began in the fourth year of Solomon's reign, which was 480 years after leaving Egypt. It is reckoned that Solomon took the throne around 971 BC thus the Exodus would have taken place around 1,450 BC. But conventional analysis dates the Exodus to the period of around 1,300 BC relative to the 430 years spent in Egypt. The anomaly that arises from the 480 years relative to the 430 years in Egypt has taxed the wisest minds throughout biblical history. But, from research presently being conducted, it is now known that the period of 430 years was plucked from the list of Noah's descendants. That period of 430 years proved to be a very significant factor in the temple calendar and the scribes may have wanted to promote its status. The issue was truly decided when the period of 476 years was found in the Messiah time-frame. Allowing for the fourth year when Solomon began to build the temple proved that the 480 years was the correct time span.

The main events and details of the staged performance of forty years wandering in the wilderness have been outlined. In the 40 year interval the Ark of the Covenant was built together with the table and the tent. The measurements of the table proved to be the same as the leap days for the periods of 20, 30 and 40 years that applied to the temple calendar and the two genealogies. Similarly, two of the measurements of the Ark matched up as leap day ratios to the measurements of Noah's ark and also provided a ratio with the cubits in Solomon's Temple and Palace. The numbers of the temple calendar had been inlaid in the Torah and preserved in customs and practices of the burnt offerings that became the central theme of Jewish worship. Thus, Moses could vacate the stage and leave it to his successors to capture and cultivate the Promised Land. But before he departed the scene it appears that the real Moses from actual biblical history was given his true recognition. He would be seen to write the Book of Laws that had their foundation in Egypt. Thus, it outlined that before he died, Moses dictated the laws and they were written on a scroll. Thereafter, he died without setting foot in the cherished land of milk and honey.

In setting the forty years scene in the wilderness the story created a longing in the Israelites to escape from that horrible desert life into the Promised Land. But the generation that came out of Egypt died before reaching that goal so their journey was never more than aspirational. It is hard to accept that the terrain of Israel could have ever been such a fertile area overflowing with milk and honey. But, from further aspects of the findings it will be shown that the notion of the Promised Land takes on a more expressive concept of the hereafter.

How the priests devised these Burnt Offerings is unknown

but it was an unusual format to bring to life the statistics of time. Perhaps, over the generations after Moses the elite priesthood devised the rituals and scenes to inculcate the numerical concepts of time into their history books. That is far more plausible than stating that all those numbers suddenly fell into place on stage in the wilderness. Those scribes must have studied all of natures characteristics be it animals, birds, bees or foliage as part of a biblical curriculum to form the imagery and symbolism of their unique language. They left a cryptic crossword with hints on the surface and deployed patterns to lead followers forever on the way to a God unknown. The faithful ones were taunted from the nursery stories through years of denial so as to arrive at the final setting with blissful aspirations of that heavenly gold medal. In that way, the sacredness of the ancient wisdom could be taught, learned and passed on from generation to generation. It would eventually become the greatest story ever told and it bewildered admirers for thousands of years. The elite few who knew the great mystery of time ceased to write sometime after the temple was destroyed for the Book of Revelation became the final chapter of the saga. Because many of the Israelites were so rebellious, the Romans slaughtered possibly half a million Jews and sects such as the Essence. In that terrible blood shed the great secret of the temple calendar also seems to have died. The Dead Sea scrolls too were lost sight of until their chance discovery in 1947.

'The entry into the Ark' (picture from King James Bible)

CHAPTER 7

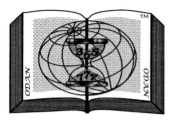

NOAH AND THE FLOOD

It may be one of the oldest nursery stories in the world but it also held another older type intellectual challenge. The story of the flood contained possibly the first numerical riddle in written existence. It stated that Noah was 500 years old when he became the father of triplets. When he was in his 600th year the flood began and it ended at the beginning of his 601st year. Yet, later in Genesis it stated that Noah's son Shem became a father when he was 100 years old, which was two years after the flood. Those two statements from the Book of Genesis are in conflict for either Noah was 498 years when his sons were born or Shem was 102 years when he became a father. It can be deduced that there was the possibility of a ± 2 years with Noah's first age thus giving it a range from 498 to 502 years as outlined in Jasher. If that riddle were not enough there were the extra challenges of the precise timings of the events with the flood. For instance, why were the dates so exact where it stated that all went into the Ark on the 17th day of the 2nd month to the very day? What was so special about the 17th day of the 2nd month? In biblical terms that period would add up to 47 days. Those two elements were just the beginning, for why did it rain for forty days and forty nights and also why did the waters rise for 150 days and then abate in another 150 days?

Biblical scholars have identified that there are two stories of the flood that coexist side by side. Both those stories have their own sets of days for when things happened and were set back to back. For instance, the waters rose for 150 days and then abated for 150 days. That chapter in Genesis allowed God to intervene somewhere in the middle of the flood story but only as if a long time period had elapsed, for it stated openly that God remembered Noah. By implication that suggestion would imply that the lord had forgotten about Noah and the actual dating system suggests that it was the case. There was also the situation where there were two separate versions of the flood. In one version there was the cosmic portrayal where the windows of the heavens were opened and the fountains of the deep were broken open. In the more earthly version it just rained for forty days and forty nights. In one story there were two of every species while in the other there were seven.

Taking on board that the 600th year of Noah began on the 1st day of the 1st month (his 601st year confirms that date) the relevant times given for the events of the flood were as follows:

Noah's 599th birthday	1st day of 1st month	
There is a 7 day delay before it rains		
		47 days
All went into the Ark and rain started:	17th day of 2nd month	---------------
It rained for 40 days and 40 nights		
Waters prevailed for 150 days		150 days
Ark rests on Mount Ararat	17th day of 7th month	---------------
God remembers Noah		74 days
Waters decrease and tops of mountains seen	1st day of 10th month	----------------
After 40 days Noah opens window of the Ark		40 days
Noah sent out a raven but it could not find dry land.		
After 7 'other' days he sends out a dove. It returns with olive branch		7 days
After 7 'other' days he sends out dove again. It does not return		7 days
601st year of Noah he removed cover off Ark	1st day of 1st month	Total = 90 days
Earth is dry		-----------------
Earth is dry	27th day of 2nd month	57 days

The surprising observation to be discerned from the layout is that indeed God did forget about Noah for there was a period of 74 days when the Ark was in the heavens. Yes, for the Ark was above the waters and eventually rested on the highest observation point of Mount Ararat. So the image of rising to the heavens was waved before our eyes.

In the sequential layout of the flood story it was ambiguous as to where the first 7 day waiting period occurred for it could have been before or after the 17th day of the 2nd month. Thereafter, the timing suggested that the 40 days and 40 nights of rain ran in parallel with the period of 150 days when the waters rose. That deduction was drawn from the fact that it was a 150 day period from 17th day of 2nd month to the 17th day of the 7th month. Yet, the waters had also abated enough during that time for the Ark rested on Mount Ararat on that day. Later in the story it appeared that time was going in reverse for apparently after another 74 days, the tops of the mountains were then seen. There was a further indication of time going in reverse where it stated at the beginning of the story that Noah was 600 years old at the time of the flood. But in fact he only reached that age at the end of the flood. Instead, the events of the flood dated back in time to early in his 600th year.

In Egypt the age span of the Pharaoh acted as a dating reference such as in the 25th year of his reign. Taking it that the age of Noah was such a calendar type reference then the beginning of his 600th year would be the day after his 599th birthday. That would have been on the 1st day of the 1st month. At the finish of the story it stated that the waters had dried up from off the earth at the beginning of Noah's 601st year which was on the 1st day of the 1st month. Then it practically repeated that statement where the earth dried but it was on the 27th day of the 2nd month, presumably of his 601st year. Therefore, it appeared that the last 57 days were superfluous to the story of the flood, which suggested there was another purpose for that period of time. But, if the events as told were actually happening in reverse it would open up a new avenue to explore the puzzle. This exercise will be rather difficult to explain but the outcome did bear fruit for the results were steeped in the numbers of the temple calendar

The starting date of where to trace the episode of the flood from was not in doubt for it was strongly emphasised to be on the 17th days of the 2nd month to the very day. The timing to the very day had echoes of the dating of the Passover and the Exodus out of Egypt to the very day. The positioning of where the waiting period of 7 days began from was practically decided for when added to the 40 days of raining they both led back exactly to the 1st day of the 1st month, which was Noah's 599th birthday. The journey continued back in time to the 17th day of the 7th month, which was 197 days back into Noah's conventional 598th year. That figure of 197 days brought two time periods together in sequence. It contained the period of 150 days when the waters rose but it also catered for the 40 days that Noah waited and the first seven 'other' days when he waited with the dove. The 47 days of abatement would explain why the Ark had time to descend and come to rest on Mount Ararat. The journey continued with the second period of 7 'other' days that Noah waited. The waters continued to recede for another 150 days. Therefore, the total time for all the periods in sequence from Noah's 599th birthday back to the 24th day of the 12th month (which was the 6th day of his 598th year) was as follows:

$$197 + 7 + 150 = 354 \textbf{ days}$$

That result was one lunar year. That outcome came as no surprise for many other enthusiasts had observed that detail before with regard to the conventional timing. Perhaps the significance of finding the lunar year was that the scribes were pointing back to when the orbits of the moon used to be the traditional method of measuring time. Or it could have been intended as a reliable checksum to position the 1st day of the 1st month as the real starting point thus making the timing from then on in whole years. That aside, it was sufficient to say that the earth was dry and it was reasonable to assume that Noah lifted the cover off the Ark on the 1st day of the 1st month of his 598th birthday.

It was important to look at the philosophical message that was emerging, which had religious overtones of the afterlife. The Ark had risen above the earth till all the land vanished beneath the waves. Thereafter, Noah and his family were ascending into the heavens and so the Bible could reliably state that Noah walked with God. Noah and his family would have had the most spectacular views of the heavens and the stars would have seemed as close as apples on a tree. Therefore, just consider the image of the Ark in the light of Egyptian belief of life in the hereafter. The dead Pharaoh was ferried by boat across the heavens accompanied by animals and food for the afterlife. The journey was to the great celestial river of the Milky Way, which was the heavenly version of the river Nile. There was also a comparison to be made in the Bible itself about travelling back in time. That was with the episode where King Hezekiah lived another 15 years when Isaiah arranged to have the clock of Ahaz turned back by ten degrees. That confirmed that putting the clock back was related to life and death issues. The journey in the Ark was to overcome death and in the earthly scene below time moved onwards and the inhabitants perished. In contrast the Ark travelled back in time and its inhabitants escaped to the heavens. Then the new time began and so it was correct for the Bible to state that Shem became a father two years after the flood.

The next step was to establish how time was going to be measured from the new beginning and naturally it would be expected that the temple year could be the eminent factor. The biblical year in the flood comprised of twelve months of 30 days each thus giving a total of 360 days. There was still what appeared to be that superfluous period from the 1st day of the 1st month of Noah's 601st year to the 27th day of the 2nd month (57 days) in what had become two years after the flood. The period of two years and the 57 days added up in sequence as follows:

$$360 + 360 + 57 = 777$$

The temple year in all its glory emerged to time out the new beginning against the backdrop of the heavens.

There was still some more aftershocks to encounter with the flood for Noah had lost two years of his age. The roll on affect would reverberate back in time with the result that Noah would have been 498 years old when he became the father of triplets. That would reduce the total of the first ages of Adam's generations by two years. That total added up to 1,556 years so the new total would thus be 1,554 years. The figure of 1,554 years was recognisable as two periods of 777 years for it was encountered in the analysis of the numbers of the tribes of Israel. It proved to be also 131 orbits of Jupiter. Therefore, the change in time caused by the flood introduced the factor of twice 777 years being in harmony with the heavenly body of the biggest planet Jupiter. The side affects of the flood continued for the total of the first ages of Adam's generations and Noah's descendants then added up in sequence to 1,554 + 390 = 1,944 years. That total of 1,944 years proved to be 66 orbits of the heavenly luminary of Saturn with just 77 leap days to harmonise with solar time. Finally, it was time to close the door on the story of the Ark by outlining that Noah's new first age of 498 years when added to the first ages of his own descendants resulted with 498 + 390 = 888 years. That number of 888 was not just a coincidence for the total of the numbers, optimal numbers and articles utilised to mean one in Chapter 8 of Genesis relating to the flood also added up to 888.

Many Bible enthusiasts view the number 888 as representing Jesus so why was it detectable twice with Noah? It was decided to multiply the two numbers of 888 together and test the total to see if any particular time period was evident. The result was spectacular and brought about the closest harmonisation between multiples of the solar year, orbits of Jupiter and one constellation of the Zodiac as follows:

888 × 888 = 788,544 **That number as day was the**
equivalent of 2,158.96 years.

4,332.59 × 182 = 788,531.28 **That number as days was**
just 12 leap days less
than 888 × 888 or 788,544 days.

Therefore, by counting the days in lots of 888 days, the ultimate harmonisation of solar time, the main luminary of Jupiter and the fixed stars of the constellations could be achieved. It only required a reduction of 12 leap days to intersect exactly with 182 orbits of Jupiter and an addition of 379 days to target the solar period of 2,160 years, which was the length of one constellation. Because 888 was just one step up from 777 a closer look was taken at the ages of Lamech. Surprisingly, his first age was 182 years, which was the same number as the orbits of Jupiter outlined in the equation above. It may have been just an innocent coincidence but Lamech's second age at 595 years was checked and it proved to be 25 orbits of Jupiter to within 25 leap days. It had been discovered earlier in the research that the first two ages of Adam at 130 years and 800 years when multiplied resulted with 24 orbits of Jupiter with just 17 leap days. Therefore, the planet Jupiter had featured three times in the ages of Adam and Noah and by association the number 888 and 777 had their relationship bonded together.

Travelling back in time would suggest that the earth would reverse its rotation to an anticlockwise motion as well as its orbital rotation around the sun. Such images fuel the imagination and create endless possibilities that are normally found in science fiction. Tackling this ancient puzzle had resolved many mysteries surrounding the story of the flood but it had also introduced its own peculiar time warp. That position arose because the total of the first ages of Adam's generations had changed to 1,554 years. Noah was in his 600th year when the flood began, which meant that it was 99 years after he became the father of triplets. Therefore, the total period from the birth of Adam to Noah at 597 years old was now 1,653 years. That period of 1,653 years was 777 temple years or 777 days by 777 times and off course it was the same period as the Messiah time-frame. But, because time was going in reverse it created that time warp that made it unclear as to when the 1,653 years ended. Throughout Noah's conventional 598th year the clock went back so that period was on another plane. Yet, it would appear from the figures that the new time began from the 1st day of the 1st month when Noah lifted the cover of the Ark and was measured with the temple year as previously outlined with the 360 + 360 + 57 = 777 days.

Those findings so far were the opening shots over the bow of the Ark for the next key to unlock the code and reveal the true value of the time periods was to hand. It was discovered in Chapter 4 of the Book of Ezekiel. The linkage to Ezekiel was pre-arranged by the scribes for the prophet had been the first to openly declare the importance of the special number of 390 days. Noah's descendants added up to 390 years. One was in days while the other was in years. The wording of the reference in Ezekiel seemed to have taken that position on board where it outlined:

"For I have laid upon thee the years of their iniquity, according to the number of days, three hundred and ninety days: so shalt thou bear the inequity." Ezekiel 4: 5

It was somewhat like the expression from the New Testament that the period of 1,000 years was like one day for with Ezekiel the years of the inequity were like 390 days. The statement went on to cite:

"thou shall bear the iniquity of the house of Judah forty days; I have appointed thee each day for a year." Ezekiel 4:6

In the reverse of the application of 390 days, the period of 40 days was to be taken as one day each for a year. It was time to return to the flood where the period of 40 days was central to the plot.

It stated in the Book of Genesis that it rained for 40 days and 40 nights. The reason for it expressing both the day and the night may have been to declare that it was for the complete solar day and not just the daylight hours. From the findings it also appears that the biblical scribes were using that presentation of days and nights to convey that 40 days and 40 nights overshot into a part of the 41st day. Biblical time measurements appear to have started from the evenings so the overshoot beyond the last day of a period was possible. Those details would be just colourful embroidery were it not for the profoundness of taking the period of 40 days and applying it as leap days of the temple calendar. The system to convert those days to years with the temple calendar formula was quite simple. The religious imperative was to measure time in a straight line direction and the basic periods were 100 and 1,000 solar years and the later measurement was found in the Messiah time-frame. There were 47 temple years of 777 days in 100 solar years with just a shortage of 5.2 leap days to be added on. In whole days that would be 50 leap days every 1,000 years to synchronise time. But to keep the calendar totally accurate an extra fraction of 0.2 days to be catered for and it added up to 2 days in 1,000 years. In 3,000 years that would be a total of 150 leap days plus 6.6 leap days to cater for the fractions of days. Therefore, for 1,000 years the leap period was 52 days and with 3,000 years 156.6 days.

There were two principal periods of temple time that would

have aroused particular attention for they comprised totally of seven. Those were the divine heavenly periods of 777 and 7,777 years. The first of those special periods with 777 years arose where the leap days were 40 days and 40 nights. With the temple calendar formula the 40 days converted to 766 ⅓ years. To achieve the exact sacred period of 777 Temple years required just an extra half day to be added thus making it 40 ½ days. There were no fractions in the story of the flood for all time values were listed as whole numbers. The extra part of a day that was inherent in the 40 days and 40 nights period would have fulfilled that shortfall of half a day. Later it will be shown that the Biblical scribes left a cryptic crossword type clue that would help the reader cherry-pick 11 solar years extra to make up the difference between 766 years and the profound period of 777 years.

Building on that discovery with the 40 days and 40 nights it was relatively easy to divide the time periods of the flood into an earthly time of days and a cosmic heavenly time of years. The waters of the flood rose for 150 days and that would match the number of whole leap days in 3,000 years when measured with the temple 777 day year. Noah waited for what was termed seven 'other' days and that would account for the fractions of 6.6 leap days. There was the second period of waiting 150 days till the waters subsided and there was also the second period of waiting seven 'other' days thus making up the leap days for a second period of 3,000 years. The two equations were as follows:

150 + 7 days match up with 3,000 years
150 + 7 days match up with 3,000 years

The divine reflection of the waters rising and falling on earth in days was with the two periods of 3,000 years that the Ark sailed through the heavens.

There was still one period that had not yet featured which was from the 17th days of the 7th month to the 1st day of the 10th month. That was a period of 74 days. In sequence with that period was the seven days that Noah waited to send out the dove. Both those periods added up to 81 days. The reflection in Temple time of those days was 1,554 years. That total was twice the sacred time of 777 years and this was the second time it featured in the story of the flood.

It was time to conduct a final checksum on the complete period of the flood in days and its reflection in the arc of heavenly time that was symbolised by the mystical figure of the rainbow. It was shown earlier that the flood ended on the 24th day of the 12th month and it was reasonable to assume that Noah lifted the cover off the Ark six days later on new years' day of the 1st day of the 1st month which was his birthday. The comparison with the 24th day of the 12th month and Christmas day on the 25th day was rather ironic particularly when the difference of one day could be accounted for by the vagaries of when a day actually began. But the task on hand was the final checksum and the assumption that the episode of the flood ended when he lifted of the cover on the 1st day of the 1st month was about to be proven. The flood began on the 17th day of the 2nd month of Noah's 600th year and time went in reverse from then till the equivalent of Noah's 598th birthday on the 1st day of the 1st month. The periods involved in days added up as follows:

7 days	waited for the rain to start
40 days and 40 nights	it rained till the 1st day of the 1st month
197 days (150 + 40 + 7 'other' days)	from 1st day of 1st month to 17th day of 7th month
150 days	waited for waters to recede till 17th day of 12th month
7 'other' days	waited to send out dove again on 24th day of 12th month
6 days	waited till Noah's birthday on the 1st day of the 1st month

Total = 407 days

Taking on board the possibility of an error of a day could be expected in the ancient way of counting with respect to the starting date, the period of 407 days was converted to its representative yearly value and it proved to be the divine temple related period of 7,777 years.

Discussion

In his book "Who Wrote the Bible" the author Friedman separated the two different stories of the flood and identified one of the original authors as J and the other as P. He outlined that J was the historical author while P was a priestly source that made the insertions many centuries later. The numerical contribution from the author J was that it rained for 40 days and 40 nights. In contrast, the priestly author P gave all the dates of the months when the flood occurred together with Noah's age at 600 years and the reference to his 600th year. P also outlined that the waters rose for 150 days and receded for 150 days. Prior to the findings of this research there was no credible explanation for P entering those days and dates in the story of the flood with their specific sets of related numbers. But, those numbers have now been shown to be the constituent building blocks of the temple calendar.

The historian Josephus outlined that 600 years was known as the Great Year and strikingly he made that claim when referring to Noah at the time of the flood. He stated that God afforded men the position to live long lives for 600 years was the period necessary to study the movement of the stars. According to Josephus, all the ancient historians were aware of the Great Year as being universal throughout the biblical lands. The period of 600 years was a milestone with the temple calendar for it required a temple month to be added to synchronise 282 temple years with 600 solar years. Thus 600 years became one of the basic building blocks of the temple calendar and five times 600 years with 3,000 years required five temple months to be added. There were two periods of 3,000 years and noticeably they were extracted out of the multiplications of the ages of Noah's seventh descendant Serug. His first age was 30 years while his second age was 200 years and those two periods multiplied out to 6,000 years. But those periods of twice 3,000 years and twice five temple months would soon be encountered again in the forthcoming analysis of the numbers in the Book of Revelation.

Without the application of the temple calendar the dates and periods of Noah and the flood would be still another biblical unsolved mystery. It is evident that the Ark itself floating above the earth was a symbol of the Messiah time-frame. That time-frame had a virtual concept that also floated above mere mortals. Eventually, the Ark came to rest on its anchor point of Mount Ararat while the Messiah time-frame was anchored on earth with the reign of Tiberius in the Roman calendar and in the heavens with the Star of Bethlehem. The flood story with the artistic brush strokes of temple time had its own peculiar heaven and earth image. On earth the leap days were anchored while the years compassed the sky like the apex of a vast wiper sweeping out a rainbow arc of the heavens.

Even today, the highway through the desert is just a remote by-road.

CHAPTER 8

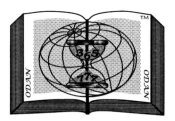

FORTY DAYS AND FORTY NIGHTS
IN THE HEAVENS

In the whole Bible there were four people that had an experience which lasted forty days and forty nights. Those people were Noah, Moses, Elijah and Jesus. Noah walked with God and also sailed up to the heavens, Elijah ascended to those same heavens in a fiery chariot so the way was well prepared for Jesus to follow suit. Moses, Elijah and Jesus were isolated during that forty days and nights period fasting, or without the need for food. Time stood still with Joshua or the clock of Ahaz went in reverse for Hezekiah to live longer. But those three amigo's of Moses, Elijah and Jesus were witnessed by three apostles to have stood side by side. Despite having lived in eras so many centuries apart, they were observed transfigured together. The 40 days and 40 nights when expressed in temple time was shown earlier to be the reflection of that chosen 777 year period. Placing that 777 year period in context with those four biblical superstars would suggest it was a gateway to the heavens with 40 days and 40 nights below reflecting 777 years in the beyond. The temple calendar had opened many doors and now it was necessary to investigate if there were common bonds between Noah, Elijah, Moses and Jesus.

It soon transpired that the four figures appear to have been linked together over the ages by a biblical cord. The story of

Noah in the Ark cemented with pitch, with it raining for 40 days and 40 nights has already been described so only the characteristics with the other figures will be identified. Moses was the next person in line and his entry into the world was rather unusual. The baby Moses in a basket made of papyrus and cemented with pitch sailing forlorn down the waters of the mighty river Nile. It was the first such boat scene since the episode with Noah's Ark floating on the waters towards the heavens. The likeness was even more relevant for to the Egyptians, the Nile mirrored the Milky Way in the heavens where the dead were ferried by boat to the afterlife. In comparison, the baby Moses was on a life and death choice of survival due to an edict by Pharaoh that all male children were to be killed. The next common bond with Moses was the second biggest episode by water in the Bible after the flood with his miraculous parting of the Red Sea. The Red Sea being divided and the Israelites marching through again created a more mystical image relative to the heavens being parted by the grand street of the Milky Way. The flood wiped out all inhabitants on earth while the Red Sea closed its waters and drowned Pharaoh's army. In identifying the linkages between Noah, Moses, Elijah and Jesus it was necessary to also watch out for specific numbers that correlated to each of them. This type of exercise would have no real validity unless the comparative numbers were really stark or were part of an overall pattern. In the first such examination it transpired that there was one common number to link the two episodes of Noah with the flood and Moses with the Red Sea, which was the number 600. Noah was 600 years old at the time of the flood while Pharaoh's chariots numbered 600.

The next linkage with Noah and Moses was with numbers relative to the dimensions of the two Arks. Noah's Ark was 300 cubits long, 50 cubits wide and 30 cubits high. In contrast the Ark of the Covenant was 2 ½ cubits long, 1 ½ cubits wide and 1 ½ cubits high. Two of the measurements were in direct proportion to the year-to-leap-day ratio of the temple calendar. That is where the 50 cubits of Noah's Ark if applied as years would equate to the 2 ½ cubits of the other Ark relative to leap days. Likewise, the 30 cubits of Noah's Ark when applied as years would equate to the 1 ½ cubits of the other Ark relative to leap days. The verification pattern of two witnesses had again sufficed. Moses ascended up onto Mount Sinai for 40 days and 40 nights (777 years) to speak to the Lord and receive the Ten Commandments. Egypt was thus left behind while the Israelites headed for the Promised Land.

That theme with water continued where Moses struck a rock with his staff and water poured forth. Perhaps the incident with the water from the rock seemed unrelated but it may have had a rather inverse meaning with the flood. Consider the situation with Moses trying to placate possibly two million people together with their vast life stock all thirsting for water. Those pining onlookers needed a flood of water to quench there thirst. Instead, Moses produced water from tapping a rock that was akin to a village pump. Moses made those two fundamental burnt offerings that comprised of those numbers 117 and 217. In contrast, Noah made the very first burnt offering to the lord who liked its aroma. Moses reached the river Jordan after 40 years wandering through the wilderness but was not allowed cross over into the Promised Land. Instead, he was shown that land of milk and honey from a mountain before he died. He was buried in Moab but the Bible outlined that the whereabouts of his grave was unknown. The next similarities were between Noah and Elijah.

Noah released a raven when the waters were drying up but it found no place to land. It would appear that it flew down through history for a flock of ravens arrived and fed Elijah while he was at a brook that was drying up. There was a drought for three years throughout Israel but finally, Elijah intervened and a cloud appeared over the sea. The cloud grew till the sky got dark and as with the flood, it poured rain. The numerical link between

Noah and Elijah was with the numbers 450 and 950, which were Noah's 2nd and final ages. Elijah faced down 450 prophets of Baal and the 400 prophets of Asherah. There were another 100 prophets hiding in two caves making 950 prophets in all. Thus, the 450 prophets of Baal and the total of all the prophets at 950 conveniently matched up as numbers with Noah's 2nd and final age. There were 100 prophets hiding and aptly enough there was also a silent 100 evident in the narrative of Noah. After Noah was 500 years old was cited together with his 600th year. It finally stated that after the flood Noah lived 350 years. And all the days of Noah were 950 years and he died. The period of 100 years between 350 and 450 years was silent.

The next link was between Moses and Elijah. It was curios that Elijah who was no fan of King Ahab still advised him from the top of Mount Carmel while looking out to sea to:

"Hitch up your chariot and go down before the rain stops you."
Kings I 18:44

Like Pharaoh with his chariots at the dramatic events when Moses parted the Red Sea, Elijah was creating a similar type image except he was warning the king to go down in his chariot before the rain stopped him. The angels of the lord fed Elijah to prepare him for a journey to mount Horeb. He then travelled forty days and forty nights presumably fasting all the way. That journey by Elijah created a direct link back to Moses with the period of forty days and forty nights it took him to walk to the mountain of Horeb. It appeared that Elijah had returned to follow in the footsteps of Moses. At the beginning of the Book of Deuteronomy Moses was breaking camp to leave mount Horeb on the first day of the eleventh month of the fortieth year. There was an associated sentence that even the Biblical translators saw as out of place for they inserted it within brackets as follows:

(It takes eleven days to go from Horeb to Kadesh Barnea by the Mount Seir road.) Deut. 1:2

There was the 11th month as cited with the 40 years and there was 11 days in the statement in brackets. Those were two of the natural time periods with the solar day and lunar month. The third one that was missing was the solar year or in this example 11 years to correspond to 11th month and 11 days. The reason for the cryptic anomaly could therefore be that 11 solar years was being signalled for it would be the correct period to convert the 40 days and 40 nights to 777 years. (40 days converted to 766 years and another 11 years was required to reach 777 years)

The contest between the false prophets and Elijah involved a burnt offerings being made by each party of a bull. Elijah challenged that they should call on their respective Gods to light the sacrificial fire. The prophets of Baal cried and danced with frenzy but their offering remained unlit. In contrast, Elijah saturated the dead bull and the wood in water but yet God sent flame from heaven that ignited the offering. Noah ascended to the heavens in the Ark whereas Elijah did not die but was carried off into the heavens on a fiery chariot. Elijah brought a young man back from the dead.

The raven had linked Noah with Elijah but our sea captain had also released a dove and the third time it never returned. It would appear that it flew right down through the spans of time to land on the head of Jesus who was noticeably getting baptised with water. The dove had earlier returned to Noah after its second trip with an olive branch so the sign of peace was offered. That sign of peace would signify the Peace Offering of 2 oxen, 5 rams, 5 goats and 5 lambs that proved to be the number 2,555, which as days was seven solar years of 365 days. That period of 7 years almost made a full house with the 777 and 7,777 years that had already been encountered in this analysis of the flood. The olive branch identified with Moses who presided over the Peace Offerings and with Jesus who was the ambassador of peace.

Noah and water are synonymous because of the flood. But Noah later planted a vineyard but became his own best customer where he got so drunk on the wine that he passed out naked. In contrast Jesus changed water into wine at the wedding feast of Canaan. That linkage with the water and wine perhaps was the real reason why the comment was made about keeping the good wine till last. Jesus was stated to have walked on water and calmed the storm that may have caused a flood. After his resurrection, Jesus was reputed to have ascended up to the heavens. There was one final link between Noah and Jesus that justified the reason for the bond between the two men. The Book of Revelation acknowledges that its writing was influenced by Jesus and it will be shown that the book contained many of the same building blocks of the temple calendar numbers that were found in the episode of the flood.

There were also some very strong similarities between the event surrounding Moses and Jesus. Just like at the time of Moses, all male new born children were condemned to be slain. The mother of Moses hid her child for three months while Mary on getting pregnant went away to live with her cousin Elizabeth for three months. Moses escaped out of Egypt with the Exodus whereas Jesus escaped into Egypt. The links between Elijah and Jesus are also evident. Elijah brought a young man back from the dead while Jesus raised Lazarus from the dead and also he brought to life a young girl who he said was sleeping.

It would appear that the message of the forty days and forty nights linking Noah, Moses, Elijah and Jesus was conveying that there were periods of 777 years between them. There were two such periods of 777 years with the new adjusted total of the first ages of Adam's generations at 1,554 years. While those incredible ages of Adam's generations and Noah's Descendants served a multifunctional purpose, their numbers were not a direct part of the calendar system to date the epochs of the Bible. However, the one overall dating source of the whole Bible was with Luke's Gospel and it listed 77 generations leading from Jesus back to Adam and then God. The 76 generations from the 30 year old Jesus back to Adam at the common age of 30 years added up to 2,280 years. The name of the 77th generation was listed as God but the supreme deity could hardly be subjected to the 30 year criterion?

It was not essential to superimpose the three periods of 777 years onto Luke's genealogy for each method stood on there own merit. There was an added dimension to the thrice 777 years, which was with the burnt offerings from whence they came. Noah made a burnt offering and the odour from it very much pleased God personally. Moses made the first official burnt offerings that incorporated the animal formations and numbering schemes. Elijah challenged the 450 prophets of Baal to ignite a burnt offering supernaturally. Those prophets failed but, in contrast Elijah drowned the burnt offering in water but yet was successful in having it consumed by fire from heaven. So when it came to Jesus the expectation was to find a burnt offering. Instead he offered up the last supper where he presented bread and wine as his body and blood. His was acting in accord with the words of Isaiah who said that the blood and fat of animals were detestable and to wash your hands of such things. Thus, the bread and wine came to symbolise the burnt offerings which were no longer necessary because the 777 temple years had expired.

It was outlined earlier that the Egyptians believed that the Milky Way was the heavenly reflection of the river Nile and viewed it as the afterlife where the Gods dwelt. The Israelites came from Egypt and were escaping to the Promised Land of milk and honey. Could it be possible that the Promised Land of Milk had a metaphorical meaning for the hereafter relative to it being an abbreviation for the Milky Way? That premise would be mere folly if there were not the tables of the heavens from these findings to support that concept. But it was how the image of tables was conveyed in the higher language that was admirable. In all of natures picturesque ways to convey a concept, what more perfect example of the honeycomb could there be to display the structure of mathematical tables? The honeycomb retains that structure and can be viewed today as it was at the time of Moses et al. The scribes even went further to highlight the concept of tables with the housing of the Ark of the Covenant. The Ark rested on a table that was 2 cubits long, 1 ½ cubits wide and 1 cubit high. Those measurements, if taken as leap days, were directly proportional to the 40 and 30 years of Mathew's and Luke's genealogies and the 20 year linear blueprint of the temple calendar.

The Promised Land of milk and honey encapsulating the Egyptian belief in the afterlife in the heavens of the Milky Way (milk) with the numerical highway to navigate to that meridian contained in the honeycomb tables (honey). The clues were left for us to follow with Samson finding the hive of bees in the carcass of the lion that he killed. He took the honey from the lion's carcass and brought it home to his family. The main periods and numbers in the story of Samson were 40 years relative to the Philistines being in power, 20 years that he was in public life and 30 cloaks from 30 companions which he won by combat to pay a wager. Those were the numbers of the Messiah time line with the genealogies and also with their ratios of the table measurements that the Ark of the Covenant rested on. There was another exploit with honey with respect to Jonathan who ate the honeycomb despite there being an edict of death for anyone touching that substance for food. Finally, John the Baptist lived on wild honey in the desert wilderness.

From the common bonds between Noah, Moses, Elijah and Jesus it was possible to reinforce the issue of the Promised Land being a metaphor for the hereafter. It was perhaps with Enoch where the first sign of the hereafter was evident. Enoch, who had that solar year number of 365, did not die for he walked with

God 'who took him.' The Bible also stated that Noah walked with God and in that regard he sailed up above the earth to the heavens in the Ark. In contrast, Moses was not allowed cross the river Jordan into the Promised Land but could only view it from a mountain. However, he did equate the Promised Land with the heavens as outlined in the Book of Deuteronomy where it stated:

"Thou art to pass over Jordan this day, to go in to possess nations greater and mightier than thyself, cities great and fenced up to heaven." Deut. 9:1

The statement of 'cities fenced up to heaven' raised the spectre of the city in the sky as outlined earlier with the Milky Way as its great street. To compound the issue the priests with Joshua took twelve stones from the river Jordan when the waters parted to let them pass over into the Promised Land. Those twelve stones bear the hallmarks of the twelve signs of the Zodiac that were embedded in those honeycomb tables. Centuries later, Elijah retraced the footsteps of Moses travelling 40 days and nights to the mount Horeb, the mountain of God. Something strange then happened for Elijah parted the waters of the river Jordan and went across casting aside his cloak. He thus entered the Promised Land and was immediately taken up to heaven in a fiery chariot. From this train of investigation the ending with Elijah was certainly making a definite statement. The mighty Moses divided the waters of the Red Sea and the whole population of the Exodus walked across but they never got to enter into the Promised Land. Pharaoh's 600 chariots drowned in the Red Sea while Elijah gave warning to save King Ahab in his chariot. In contrast, Elijah parted the Jordan River and ascended into heaven on a mystical chariot. The path was thus well prepared for Jesus who also ascended into heaven forty days after the Resurrection without the need of a chariot.

Pyramids

CHAPTER 9

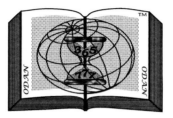

THE PYRAMIDS

It is known that the Babylonians were the most sophisticated mathematicians of the old world and had devised reference tables to speed up the various forms of computations. Yet, their mathematics was to the base sixty which ironically is still very much evident with the measurement of time. For instance, they measured time by counting 60 minutes in an hour. But they are not credited with using the base ten which we employ in our metric system. That type of arithmetic requires that we use a zero in the counting system when going beyond the single digits of one to nine. Without delving too far into the technicalities of arithmetic it is suffice to say that the findings outlined so far fly in the face of contemporary knowledge about the abilities of those ancient people. The Babylonians adhered to a lunar/solar calendar and therefore, the one true God of solar time was not within their achievements. Yet, they excelled in astronomy, astrology and numerology. Only the Egyptians in that part of the world had progressed to utilise a solar calendar. But they stuck to a 365 day long solar year and ignored the importance of that extra fraction of a day. That extra fraction was necessary to be factored in to synchronise the measurement of time exactly. The catch-cry of the Gospels of "Out of Egypt I have called my son" seemed like a visual pun on son (sun), especially as it appeared to be where the solar dimension was imported from by the Israelites.

'There was something extraordinary about the genealogy in Luke's Gospel, which had 76 names dating back to Adam and with the 77th generation shown as God. By applying the period of 30 years it meant that the time measurement back to Adam was in the region of the year 2,250-2,280 BCE. That date was not far removed from the completion of the great pyramid. There was a particular body of opinion who accepted that the pyramids were designed to comply with an astronomical agenda. In the 19th century the Scottish astronomer, Charles Pizza Smyth published a book which maintained that the lost wisdom of Enoch was contained in the measurements of the great pyramid. Perhaps the theme by Smyth et al had scientific merits but his work was discredited for mixing biblical prophecy with science. The research findings so far were perhaps the most revealing and controversial set of biblical results ever discovered. Therefore, to switch from the biblical written format to the most mysterious solid building in the world was tempting fate. Moses came out of Egypt so it was time to follow in his footsteps and examine the signposts that he left.

It was pointed out in Chapter 3 of this book that Moses was shown t*he earlier and later history of the division of all the days* on Mount Sinai. The numbers of the two censuses of the tribes of Israel proved to be a disguise and were shown to represent days. That would have been the later history of the days so the focus was on the earlier historical version of days. The pyramids were built at least one thousand years before Moses so perhaps that was where Kainam had found the ancient writing of the watchers? The Book of Jubilees referred to the writing on a rock but elsewhere in that book it referred to the pyramids as those pillars of stone.

To understand the calendar blueprint and how it might be encased in the measurements of the pyramids it was necessary to get down to the finer basic details. The actual system employed to count the days with the temple calendar was considered to be all in ones up to the number of 111 days. Thereafter, the counting continued with 222 days then 333, 444, 555, 666 and 777 days. The noticeable factor about 111, 222, 333 and 666 was that they all return to the same anniversary date every 31 years. Therefore, those four numbers were of the same value relative to a calendar. It was outlined earlier that there were eight burnt offerings but that only seven applied to the exercise with the temple calendar. The very first burnt offering was set out in Chapter 7 of the Book of Numbers but it did not stand on its own. Rather it was included in a matrix with several other offerings such as the Peace and Sin offering. That burnt offering comprised of one bullock, one ram and one lamb, which when presented in tabular form revealed the following:

Bullocks	Rams	Lambs
1	1	1

In that tabular format the number 111 was evident. From the results of the earlier research findings it was likely that the new number of 111 was intended to represent days. It seemed to have been presented in Chapter 7 of Numbers as a basic numerical element for counting the days. The findings from the burnt offerings, particularly the 777 as days verified that position. But the scribes left a marker to show that those offerings in Chapter 7 of Numbers had a time related dimension. That was where the deciphered number of 2,555 was revealed from the peace offering with its inherent period of seven years of 365 days. What was required to complete the 111 day timeframe was its counterpart of 31 years. It was not difficult to find for if the men in the two censuses represented days then the years were likely to be associated with royalty. In Chapter 12 of the Book of Joshua it outlined the names of the kings that were slain in the capture of the Promised Land. The names were listed as follows:

The king of Jericho	one
The king of Ai	one
The king of Jerusalem	one

The sequence of names continued and the numbers were listed as one, one, one until they stopped at the king of Tirzah totalling 31 kings in all. It was a the number 31 encased in an exercise of counting one by one and the layout in the Gideon Bible make it a perfect example of the actual counting system

Therefore, the two elements of the counting system with 111 as days and 31 as years were clearly identified. There were several offerings made by each of the leaders of the twelve tribes the first being a silver charger weighing 130 shekels. That offering introduced three main features. The first feature was that 130 was also the first large number in the Bible it being the age of Adam. It was also the approximate period when a leap day had to be subtracted to keep the 365 ¼ day solar year in check. The third feature was that the 130 introduced the concepts of weights and measures with the shekels. Moses and the Israelites had just come out of Egypt when those offerings were made so weights and measures did have a particular significance. It was tempting to examine the dimensions of the great pyramid for evidence of the temple calendar. Unlike previous investigations, this was the first time that anyone had gone looking for the blueprint of the temple calendar in the pyramid measurements.

The length, breadth and height of the Kings and Queens were targeted and their cubic measurements were as follows:

	Length	Breadth	Height
Kings chamber	19.96	9.98	11.09
Queens chamber	10.95	9.98	11.87

Numbers and arithmetic can perplex the brain till coincidence becomes certainty. But those measurements from the two chambers as listed above were pregnant with the numbers of the temple calendar. Just like the earlier outline with the measurements of Solomon's temple, those measurements or combinations thereof held the same values. The principal measurements of the two genealogies and temple time were with the numbers 20, 30 and 40 relative to years. In the pyramid measurements above the numbers of cubits outlined had the basics to form those very same numbers with the following:

- 19.96 (20) cubits as the length of the Kings chamber

- 19.96 + 9.98 = 29.94 (30) for the length and breadth of the Kings chamber.

- 19.96 + 9.98 + 9.98 = 39.92 (40) for the length breadth of the kings chamber and the breadth of Queens chamber.

To make the observations more pronounced, the breadth of both chambers was the same at 9.98 cubits, which would compel the mind to combine them to 20 cubits. The measurements of Solomon's temple were as follows:

- Breadth 20 cubits. The combined breadth of the kings and Queens chamber was 9.98 + 9.98 = 19.96 (20) cubits. The length of the Kings chamber was also 20 cubits.

- Height 30 cubits. The length and breadth of the Kings chamber was 19.96 + 9.98 = 29.94 (30) cubits.

- Length of the courtyard 40 cubits. Kings chamber length and the combined breadth of the two chambers was 19.96 + 9.98 + 9.98 = 39.92 (40) cubits.

By any standards those three results were remarkable for they matched up with the principal numbers of 20, 30 and 40 years that were outlined earlier with the temple calendar. Those were also the main numbers used by Jacob when he presented his brother Esau with livestock to compensate for the wrong he had done to him.

The next part of the investigation involved multiplying the length, breadth and height of the Kings and Queens chambers in the great Pyramid. There were some amazing results as follows:

- The totals of the multiplied cubits for the breadth by the height for the Kings chamber came to 110.67, which was practically 111 cubits.

- The length by the height came to 221.15, which was practically 222 cubits.

- The overall total of the multiplied results for both chambers added up to 888.82, which was practically 888 cubits.

- The length by the height of the Queens chamber came to 129.97, which was practically 130 cubits.

Those numbers were the blueprint of the temple calendar. The margin of error was such that a slight subsidence in the pyramid would have caused the inaccuracy. In the way the numbers were presented it appeared like a pattern with 111 then 222 and adding the two gave 333 (111 + 222) with the 444, 555, 666 and 777 silent and ending on 888. But, there was even more substantiating evidence to confirm the conclusions that were emerging. It was outlined above that counting of the days in lots of 111 and 222 days results in returning to the same anniversary date every 31 years. To compliment that bigger picture the number of cubits with the length and height of the Kings chamber that multiplied out to 222 cubits, had themselves added up to 31 cubits. That result was reinforced by the second total of 31 cubits, which was the total of the two lengths of both chambers.

The length and height of the Queens chamber had multiplied out to 130 cubits which was the same number as the number of shekels in the offerings that were made in Chapter 7 of Numbers. It was also the first large number in the Bible with the age of Adam. It looked like Moses from his place of privilege in Pharaoh's household had known the secret of the Great Pyramid. To put the findings on a firmer footing the details of the most dynamic building of the Bible with Solomon's temple were again examined. The detailed instructions for building the temple were outlined in Chapter 6 of the Book of Kings1 and the findings revealed the following comparisons:

- Cubits from the Great Pyramid = 111 + 222 = 333 cubits

- Total cubits in the chapter on building Solomon's temple = 333 cubits

- Total of multiplied and added cubits in the two Pyramid chambers = 888 cubits

- Total of the numbers and optimal numbers in Chapter 6 of Kings1 = 888

Those two findings together with the total of the cubits at 333 and the totals of the numbers at 888 were spectacular. It was outlined earlier that the adjusted ages of Adam and Noah's descendants added up to 888. Also, all of the numbers, optimal numbers etc. in Chapter 8 of the Book of Genesis, which described the flood abating came to a total of 888. So the number 888 was no single swallow when it came to biblical listings. That the pyramid contained the measurements of the heavens was also evident for the notable number of 888 had been dimensioned into those two chambers. It was shown in the chapter above with Noah that 888 multiplied by 888 produced the equivalent result as 182 orbits of Jupiter and one constellation of the Zodiac. It was a very good example of where the solar year, the orbit of Jupiter and the constellations were in harmony.

The normal calculation was to multiply the length by the breath or height. Going one step further all the other measurements of the two chambers were first multiplied by the length of the Kings chamber and then by its breadth and then by its height. Similarly, the other measurements were multiplied by the length and then by the height of the Queens chamber. There were five such multiplications possible for the two breadths were the same for both chambers thus creating a repeat of that result. The multiplied results for each of those five groups were added up individually. One of those results totalled 676.5 cubits. If that number were applied as days with the temple calendar then it matched up with half the cycle of the Zodiac at 12,960 years.

Summary

The Jewish historian Josephus had referred to two pillars of wisdom on which the statistics of the heavens had been engraved. One of those pillars was made of stone and the other of brick. Those engravings were written so as to pass onto future generations the wisdom of the ancients prior to the flood. Perhaps Josephus had acquired that knowledge from the Book of Jubilees, which had been referenced above. The results from the numbers in the two chambers of the great pyramid would suggest that it was the pillar of stone. The offerings made by each of the leaders of the twelve tribes were deciphered as 111. As each leader did the presentation the numbers would have added with 111, 222,

333...888 etc. The corresponding number of 31 was found in a counting exercise with dead kings with one, one, one etc. up to 31. That was the biblical version and there in the Kings chamber of the great pyramid the measurements had multiplied to 111 and 222 while the total came to 888. Corresponding to the 31 element was the total of the same length and height that had multiplied out to give 222. Those two measurements added up to 31. The number 130 was found in those same set of biblical offerings and also in the computations of the Queens chamber. There was the comparison of 333 and the overall checksum figure of 888 from the two chambers with the two overall totals in the building of Solomon's temple. And the square of 888 was shown to have a very special period when expressed as days. Finally there was the leap day numbers for half the length of the Zodiac at 677 found in the computations of the chambers.

Finding traces of the temple calendar in the great pyramid introduced an interesting fact. Throughout the whole Bible there is not one mention of those huge buildings. They are however mentioned in other biblical sources as the pillars of stone. Nor is the river Nile ever called by name though it is referred to as the river of Egypt. Both those factors seem rather strange when the same anonymity also applies to the name of God. Many sources point out that the rebel Pharaoh Akhenaton adopted monotheism and they make the connection as being similar to the Hebrew worship of one God. Finding traces of the temple calendar and the comparable 888 checksum in the great pyramid copper fastened the linkage and opens up a whole new debate on the origins of Jewish belief. Thus, the findings confirmed that the temple calendar was Egyptian in origin but had been acquired by the Israelites.

Ephesus

CHAPTER 10

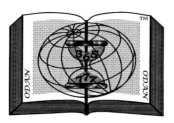

REVELATION

The Bible suddenly is an explorer's dream full of teasing clues, daunting puzzles and rewarding nuggets. The key to explore this mysterious ancient wonder is the temple calendar and now the Book of Revelation will become the classroom topic. For almost two thousand years the words, numbers and imagery in that book have been the ammunition for prophets of doom to invoke hell fire and damnation threatening that the end is nigh. But these findings will now show that Revelation was the road map of the temple calendar. Many of those provocative symbols were merely signposts to direct us where its constituent elements were to be found in the Bible. The opening lines of the Book of Revelation begin with the words:

"The Revelation of Jesus Christ which God gave unto him, to show unto his servants things which must shortly come to pass.....Blessed is he that readeth, and they that bear the words of this prophecy and keep those things which are written therein: for the time is at hand." Rev 1:1:3

The time is at hand. Because the statement at the beginning of the Book of Revelation was so emphatic, it meant that a revised version of the temple calendar structure about to be revealed was the artwork of Jesus Christ. Up to now most elements of the temple calendar were found scattered throughout the various books of the Old Testament. But Jesus had obviously got the task of drawing up or presenting a more cohesive simplified version in a small book that would be called Revelation. Jesus was a carpenter by trade and the arithmetic suggested that he was gifted in the one true language of numbers and measurement. He was thus conferred for his abilities with mental arithmetic. Therefore, it should come as no surprise that the simplified fundamental elements of the temple time periods and pertinent numbers were listed in the Book of Revelation. In that regard, the assertive clues suggested that Jesus wrote out the instruction manual of the temple calendar.

The true purpose of the periods of 5 months, 42 months, 1,260 days and 6,000 years together with that very much maligned number of 666 can at last be truthfully outlined. Those periods have been the subject of every oddball theory for centuries. That number of 666 alone brought up 114,000,000 listings on the Google search engine. It took the long arm of the temple calendar to destroy all those fearful myths and show the constituent numbers to be an integral part of time measurement.

THE NUMBER 666 EXORCISED

Against the tide of public opinion, it will be shown that the number 666 was wrongfully maligned because of its innocent association with the number of a man and of a beast. The number 666 was quoted in the Book of Revelation in the context of:

And that no man might buy or sell, save he that had the mark or the name of the beast, or the number of his name.
Here is wisdom. Let him that had understanding count the number of the beast; for it is the number of a man and his number is 666.
Rev. Ch. 13 : 17 :18

Those few sentences have dominated so many agendas with the number of the beast being perceived as evil and cited as Satan, Nero or any tyrant dictator in history. Some large hotels exclude the number 666 from their room numbers and people are generally superstitious if that number appears in any transaction.

In the quotation above, the phrase "here is wisdom" prompted of Solomon who was renowned for his wisdom. Taking the prompt literally, the microscope focused on the reign of Solomon where the following statement was particularly noticeable:

Now the weight of gold that came to Solomon in one year was 666 talents of gold. 11Chron Ch 9 : 13

To find that number of 666, albeit the number of talents was a surprise reward and it gave the impetus to search further. It was therefore stimulating to come across the following statement in the Book of Ezra as follows:

The children of Ad-on-ikam six hundred, sixty and six Ezra Ch 1 : 13

The descendants of a man called Ad-on-ikam were 666 men. Common sense would suggest that the number of a man had finally being exposed and it was nothing to do with Caesar or Satan. Ad-on-ikam was that man. But, could it be proved beyond doubt that Ad-on-ikam was the correct fellow. Either way, there was still the number of the beast to unravel. It was a whole new ball game for now the number of 666 with Solomon and Ezra together with its appearance in Revelation made up three separate listings of 666 in the Bible. Would it be outrageous to assume that the number of the beast involved three 666s and that the temple calendar would be the central focus of the mystery?

The research continued by examining the related promptings which were in the very next chapter of Revelation. Some of those helpful clues were as follows:

And I looked and lo a lamb stood on mount Sion and with him an hundred forty and four thousand , having his fathers name written in their foreheads....and before the four beasts...and they were not defiled...being the first fruits unto God and to the lamb. Rev. Ch 14 : 1 : 2 : 3 : 4

The four beasts that were not defiled was obviously pointing at the burnt offerings in Chapter's 28 and 29 of the Book of Numbers where bullocks, rams, lambs and goats of the 1st year without blemish were sacrificed. It even listed the First-fruits, which was one of the feast days when the beasts were to be sacrificed. To reinforce the issue further there was also reference in the same chapter in Revelation to smoke from a furnace invoking images that could be the setting for burnt offerings. The burning furnace, the lamb stood on Mount Sion had its parallels in Chapter 28 of Numbers where it stated:

It is a continual burnt offering, which was ordained in mount Si'nai for a sweet savour, a sacrifice made by fire unto the lord. Num. 28:6

From such high visibility landmarks it was almost certain that the excavation site of the beasts had been clearly identified. It was time to roll in the three 666s. In the previous research the numbers from the burnt offerings and the days in the Messiah time-frame had been validated as having retained their original values with the aid of checksums. That exercise catered for the prominent numbers but there were still the set of instructions involving, additions and multiplications of the numbers and fractions to be verified. Those set of instructions were outlined in Chapters 28 and 29 of the Book of Numbers where Moses made the burnt offerings that comprised of the four sacrificial beasts. Included with those sacrifices were portions of flour, oil and wine that were to be mingled with the beasts. All together, it involved a maze of numbers and computations. All the sacrifices were to be offered at their set times over the space of a year. In reality, this meant that two chapters which contained the details were in fact one joint group. It would be a daunting exercise to undertake but what could be the outcome? Might it be possible that there was a grand checksum total to verify the final count of the combined two chapters in the Book of Numbers? If so, did it involve those three 666s?

There were two different checksums to be contemplated the first of which was to validate the numbers and fractions listed in those two chapters. For instance, the authorized King James original version of the Bible cited "a several tenth deal of flour" in the two chapters of the Book of Numbers whereas the revised English Bible published by Oxford University Press 1989 had changed the instruction to "one tenth." Such a change would affect any checksum. The second type checksum would have to take on board the multiplications and additions given in the instructions so as to ascertain what number of animals and fractions of flour, wine and oil were offered in the complete year. Therefore, it was imperative that the numbers as listed could be proven to be the correct original values. That exercise would have to take on board which version of the Bible had the correct interpretation. If not, the multiplications and additions would amplify the errors and invalidate any intended checksum.

The first exercise was carried out and all the numbers as listed in Chapter 28 of the original KJV were added up. Those numbers included the numbers of beasts to be sacrificed together with the numbers of days and the optimal days of the month. i.e. Such as the 1st, 7th and 14th day. The total came to 127. The fractions were then added and the total came to 3.47. Thus, the two totals came to 127 + 3.47 = 130.47. In whole numbers that total was the same as the first age of Adam, which was also the first large number in the Bible. It was also the weight in shekels of the silver chargers made as an offering by each of the twelve tribes of Israel under the instructions of Moses. Indeed, that was the very first offering made on the very first day that Moses set up and sanctified the tabernacle and altar. But to truly decide the issue the total of 130.47 as years was eleven orbits of Jupiter. Because the orbit of Jupiter had already featured so prominently in the previous 'Infallible Numbers' checksum it was reasonable to assert that the total of 130.47 had proven the numbers and fractions to have retained their original values intact.

The exercise continued and all the numbers in Chapter 29 were added up and came to 367. Likewise, the fractions were counted and the total was 1.69. The logical course was to add the two totals but there was a twist in the puzzle. The fractions in Chapter 29 arose mainly from the offerings that had been shown to represent 117 years. That period of 117 years when measured with the temple year of 777 days had to have 1.66 days subtracted to reach the exact day. Therefore, the 1.66 days were a minus value. It was also very noticeable that 1.66 matched up very favourably with the total of the fractions at 1.69. Taking those factors on board the totals of the numbers and fractions were equated together with 367 − 1.69 = 365.31. The result was the length in days of the solar year. Because the solar year had figured so prominently in the whole research findings it seemed very likely to have been intended by the scribes as a validation checksum.

It was time to move on and find if there was indeed one overall checksum that would validate all the computations arising from the instructions given by Moses in chapters 28 and 29 of the Book of Numbers. Those instructions were followed to the letter of the law and proved to be an exercise as arduous as any cryptic crossword. There was hardly one superfluous word in those instructions but yet the calculations had to take on board that many portions of the offerings had to be repeatedly factored into the equations. Because of the fractions it was never going to be possible to achieve an exact whole number result. The totals of all the beasts to be sacrificed in a year including the fractions of flour, oil and wine were counted up for both chapters.

- The total combined result came to 1,997.08, which was practically three times the number 666.

The number of the beast had finally been resolved. Even the singular form of the word 'beast' was catered for because the result was encased in one great checksum where all the numbers of the beasts were taken as just neutral numbers. The Bible that was used to perform the exercise was the original KJV so where stands those Bibles that had altered some of the figures? That aside, the satanic myth of the number of the beast was truly exorcised.

Jesus the Mathematician

When the temple year formula of 777 days was applied to the main time periods and some of the numbers in the book of Revelation they proved to be the years and leap day periods of the sacred calendar. The time periods and relevant numbers cited in Revelation were as follows:

Time Periods		Numbers
1	day listed twice.	144
3.5	days listed twice	666
10	days	1,600
A	month	7,000
5	months	10,000 Cited twice
A	year	12,000 Cited 13 times
42	months listed twice.	144,000 Cited 3 times
1,260	days listed twice.	200,000,000
1,000	years cited six times	

The key to constructing the time table of the temple calendar was to understand the role and value of its associated intervals as distinct from the normal calendar intervals such as with the period of a month. To begin with, the temple year was 777 days long whereas the solar year is 365 ¼ days long. (365.242 days to be more precise) The biblical month was usually understood to be 30 days but, in reality, the actual calendar month would have to be 30.43 days long for twelve months to add up to 365 ¼ days. The temple month has its own value and strangely it was almost the same as the solar month though it served a different role. That role was where it served as a leap period for the specified times of 5 and 42 months. To establish the length of the temple month it was necessary to relate to its corresponding linear period, which was 600 years.

St. John's Grave

The computation was shown in the last chapter where the temple month had been revealed as the shortfall between 282 temple years and 600 solar years in the outline with Noah and the flood. From the computation, the temple month proved to be 31.3194 days long and it was almost equivalent to the actual calendar month of 30.43 days. Because of that similarity, the scribes possibly had retained that traditional name of 'month.'

There are two periods of 42 months cited in the Book of Revelation and there are also two periods of 1,260 days. Biblical scholars hold the view that the period of 1,260 days was equivalent to 42 months. But that use of repeating the same equivalent time values would have been superfluous and not conform to the principle of Jewish economy. The temple month was 31.3194 days long. However, it was likely that the more manageable period of 31 ¼ days was used so that periods of whole days could be achievable in predicting long periods of time. (That situation is similar to the fraction of a leap day with our calendar for it is rounded up to ¼ day so as to have a full leap day every four years. The inherent fractional error is corrected by foregoing a leap day every 400 years and with other longer term corrections) From the outcome of these deliberations with the temple month it can be shown that 1,260 days and 42 months have different values for the 42 months was 31 ¼ × 42 = 1,312 ½ days.

When studying at junior school we were given sequences of numbers with some of the relevant figures missing and from the pattern, we were expected to fill in the gaps. The same applied to this exercise in building the temple calendar time table for we were given some of the years and some of the days and we have just to fill in the gaps to match them up with each other respectively. There were also the neutral numbers which could be applied as time periods. It was already shown that 600 years equated to a revised month of 31.25 leap days. There were six periods of 1,000 years cited in Revelation and therefore, the first, second and third periods of the temple calendar could readily be outlined as follows:

600 years equated to 31.25 leap days

3,000 years equated to 31.25 × 5 = 156.25 leap days
which was 5 temple months

6,000 years was equated to 5 temple months
+ 5 temple months.

That was a simple exercise and it was virtually a repeat of the findings outlined previously with the flood. It appeared that Jesus had provided both the years and equivalent leap days to guide us on how to carry out the matching process with the temple calendar. There was a statement in Revelation outlining 'a year, a month, a day and an hour' in sequence. However, the period of a week was absent but there were two periods of 3 ½ days listed elsewhere in Revelation. Therefore, all the calendar time intervals of a year, month, week, day and an hour were evident. The next time interval that was examined was the period of one year of 365 ¼ days and its matching period in years was 7,000 years. It was all so convenient for there was the number 7,000 in Revelation. So both matching numbers of a year and 7,000 were already in place waiting for somebody just to tick the boxes. But, heretofore, nobody had the key formula with the temple year of 777 days to match those values of years to their respective leap days. The complete figures are shown in Table 2.

That was three of the time table periods of 3,000, 6,000 and the number 7,000 as years that had been formed from the temple calendar. By homing in on the other numbers two more matches were easily identified. Those were as follows:

The number 144 matched up reasonably with 3 ½ + 3½ days (7 days)

The number 1,600 matched up with the numbers 42 + 42 (84)

Here again, both of the matching sides of the equation were given, albeit the years being in just neutral numbers. In effect, the pattern had been made clearly evident so filling in the remaining parts of the table with its vacuum of missing numbers could begin. Because multiples of the 'month' had been already used as matches for 3,000 and 6,000 years it was reasonable to add in the principal base of 600 years and the single period of a month to the time table. It was also quite logical to add in 10,000 as years for it matched up with the periods of 5 months of 156 ¼ + 365 ¼ days (a year) = 521 ½ days

That was seven clear examples of the role of the temple year in producing the matches of years to leap days from some of the most debated numbers in the Book of Revelation. It was like child's play but there were also a few numerical riddles to be confronted. Take for instance, the very basic period of linear time of 100 years was not openly displayed. But with the knowledge of the temple calendar the 100 years was visible beneath the surface of 1,260 days and the number 666.

━━━━━━━━━━━━━━━━━━━━━━━━━━━━━━━━━━▶

Note. In the Table across relating to the Book of Revelation there are some factors to be outlined as follows: In Revelation the periods of time are arranged with 1,000 years cited six times. One third of 5 months was the number of 'leap' days for 1,000 years. The scribes had left a landmark for the 'the third part' was quoted twice in the same chapter where the 5 months were cited twice. There was also 'the fifth' at the beginning of the same chapter and when applied to the 3,000 it gave 600 years and to a 1,000 it gave 200 years. In turn, when the fifth was applied to the 200 it gave 40 years. To compliment this observation, the periods of 600, 200, and 40 years conveniently match up with the small periods of a month, 10 days and 2 days that were listed in Revelation.. There were six periods of 1,000 years, which was 6,000 years. The next two highest numbers were 7,000 and 10,000 and the liberty was taken to apply those as years. The time of 12,960 was interpreted by the author as meaning 'half a time' in the quotes from the Books of Daniel and Revelation. It is therefore included in the table and taking the cue from Revelation Ch18.6 where it states to 'double and double,' the 12,960 years was doubled to 25,920 and then to 51,840 years. To reinforce that assumption, the 42 months plus 42 were found to match with those two periods of 25,920 and 51,840 years.

Table 2: The Jesus Time Table

Years		Leap day fraction	Days	Leap periods from Revelation
20	×	0.052199	1.04	1 day
40	×	0.052199	2.08	2 days
70	×	0.052199	3.65	3.5 days
100	×	0.052199	5.22	3.5 days + 2 days
144	×	0.052199	7.52	3.5 Days + 3.5 days
200	×	0.052199	10.44	10 days
600	×	0.052199	31.32	1 Temple month
1,000	×	0.052199	52.2	10 days + 42
1,600	×	0.052199	83.52	42 + 42
2,000	×	0.052199	104.4	2d+3.5d+3.5d+10d+42+42
3,000	×	0.052199	156.6	5 Temple months
6,000	×	0.052199	313.2	Twice 5 Temple months
7,000	×	0.052199	365.393	1 Year
10,000	×	0.052199	522	1 Year + 5 Temple months
12,000	×	0.052199	626.38	2d+3.5d+3.5d+10d+42+42+5m+1y
12,960	×	0.052199	676.5	1 Year + twice 5 Temple months
25,920	×	0.052199	1,353	42 Temple months + 42
51,840	×	0.052199	2,706	Twice 42 Temple months + 42 + 42

Their respective yearly periods to return to the same anniversary date were 69 and 31 years, which was 100 years. That example demonstrates the sheer wizardly employed by the Biblical authors in presenting mental arithmetic hurdles for the reader. The matching leap days for 100 years were 5.2 leap days and 3 ½ + 2 days = 5 ½ days were listed in Revelation. The two periods were reasonably compatible especially seeing that the 5 whole days would be readily applied while the fractional part would be set aside till a full leap day would accrue in the future. The next figures in the table were the two periods of 42 months. Multiplying out the month by 42 times gave 31 ¼ × 42 = 1,312 ½ days. That period as leap days proved to be the match of 25,144 years. It fell short of one cycle of the Zodiac of 25,920 years by just 43 days. Therefore, the multiplier number of 42 bridged the gap between 25,144 and one cycle of the Zodiac of 25,920 years with a slight error in the range of 28 years or with its matching leap day period of just over one leap day. The same exercise was carried out with twice the periods of 42 months and their leap days multiplied out to two cycles of the Zodiac at 51,840 years.

The exercise continued and the relevant remaining numbers provided in the book of Revelation were utilised and their respective matching periods were added in. For example, the period of 1 day was listed and of course it was the blueprint leap day of the temple calendar for it matched up with the period of 20 years. Likewise, there was another period of a day and it was logical to match up the combined 2 days to match up with the period of 40 years. Therefore, the biblical author had provided the leap days for the principal periods of 20 and 40 years that were two of the blueprint figures of the temple calendar. In that way all of the matching numbers in the table were filled in. The number 666 and the two periods of 1,260 years could have been filled in with their matching leap days but it was perceived that those numbers served a different purpose. e.g. the function of the number 666 was already outlined above.

FROM BABYLON TO BETHLEHEM

The reference to the number 666 had led to the book of Ezra where the descendants of Ad-on-ikam had numbered 666. There was also a comparable listing of the men who returned from Babylon in the Book of Nehemiah although there were several differences with some of the figures. For instance, the men of Ad-on-ikam were numbered as 667 in Nehemiah. Was it more than just coincidence that the number 138 was listed as the number of gatekeepers in Nehemiah but as 139 in Ezra? That number 138 if applied as years, was twice the period of 69 years, which was outlined earlier as the natural recycling time for the period of 1,260 days. And 1,260 days was quoted twice in the Book of Revelation.

Therefore, the number 666 and 1,260 were represented in Ezra and Nehemiah and both had an anomaly that made them stand out. That was another two familiar signpost clues to lead us further into temptation. There was a specific group of men known as the "Men from Bethlehem," which was King David's city and where the Messiah Jesus was born. Just like with the two censuses, could those numbers listed as men be in fact representing days? If so, it would open up another long lost royal numerical tomb whose treasure lay untouched through time. The clues continued to mount up for the period of 1,000 years was cited six times in Revelation while the walls of Jerusalem that had been rebuilt by Nehemiah had earlier proven to represent 1,000 years. There was an oddity with Ezra and Nehemiah for although they lived at least 100 years apart, they were cited as being side by side in the book of Nehemiah. References to Babylon having fallen in the Book of Revelation prompted of the Jewish return from exile and of course, the numbers who were cited as coming back were listed in Ezra and Nehemiah.

In Bethlehem some things have not changed

Of the men that returned it was noticeable that the numbers of Nebo, Magbish and Elam, which were all in direct sequence were 52, 156 and 1,254. Those numbers were so obvious for they were the equivalent of the leap days for 1,000, 3,000 and 24,000 years, two of which had been set out in the table above that was derived from Revelation. Indeed, it took Nehemiah 52 days to finish the 1,000 cubit long wall of Jerusalem and now the number 52 began a sequence recognisable as temple time measurements. Because of the oddity of Ezra and Nehemiah standing side by side, the two sets of numbers from both of their books were inserted on a table side by side. In the Gideon Bible, the men were formed in their respective groups such as the men from Israel, the men from Bethlehem, the priests and Levites. The grouping of the men from Bethlehem was where the three numbers of 52, 156 and 1,254 were listed. It was decided to probe deeper into the anomalies between the two sets of figures from Ezra and Nehemiah. From the observations it appeared that there were four different groups of anomalies which were as follows:

1. There were three extra men in Ezra's list.

2. One extra man in Nehemiah's list.

3. Six of the numbers in Ezra's list were larger than the numbers in Nehemiah's list.

4. Eleven numbers in Nehemiah's list were larger than those with Ezra.

That was four sets of anomalies in all. All the numbers and the anomalies were then added up and the totals are shown in Table 3. The totals of all the men returning was listed in both books as 42,360, but that total was incorrect for the numbers in Ezra added up to 29,818 men while in Nehemiah the total proved to be 31,089 men.

The total of those anomalies was like a beacon for it was a checksum type figure at 3,655 or ten solar years. There was a slight error of three to make it exactly ten years to the very day. All of the totals of 64,562 were then checked for a checksum figure and it proved to be six orbits of Saturn to within six days. Just like the burnt offerings, the scribes had encased both the totals and the four groups of anomalies in two checksum figures that were constants and recognisable throughout history. Because of the error of three and six days in both checksum figures it was reasonable to say that the numbers in the two lists of names from Ezra and Nehemiah had retained their original values almost intact to within an error of 3 to 6 units. It was also reasonable to accept that the anomalies were deliberately arranged by the scribes to serve some particular function because they had encased their totals in a checksum value that was the equivalent of ten solar years.

Table 3: Ezra and Nehemiah, Side by Side

	Ezra		Nehemiah		Ezra	Ezra +	Neh. +	Neh		Totals
Total	29,818		31,089		854	338	1,815	648	=	64,562
Bible Totals	42,360		42,360							
Totals of the anomolies					854	338	1,815	648	=	3,655

Note. There were some problems with interpretation with some of the names for a man called Hashum was listed 17th in Ezra's list as numbering 223 but was listed 15th in Nehemiah's list as numbering 328.The names were the same so the two numbers were re- grouped and placed opposite each other. There was a man called Jorah who was listed in 16th position on Ezra's list that numbered 112 whereas in Nehemiah's list a man called Hariph who also numbered 112 was listed in 17th position. Because the numbers were the same and their positional system was in such close proximity the two names were treated as being the same person. Therefore, the numbers were re-grouped opposite each other.

The totals of the men from Bethlehem had included the numbers 52, 156 and 1,254 in direct sequence but it also contained a further surprise when the anomalies were examined, as shown in Table 4. The totals of the differences between the list of men from Nehemiah and Ezra added up to that solar year figure of 365. Those were listed as men and a man is a man, but when he wears a crown like 365, he is a king. Therefore, the number of 365 appeared to be a symbolic halo and perhaps indicated that the numbers bore values that were in fact days. But that finding was even more than symbolic for as leap days, the number of 365 matched up with 7,000 years. It was the same match of numbers that was encountered earlier from Table 2 as derived from the Book of Revelation. Another of the totals of the men from Bethlehem came to 104, which so readily was the equivalent of the leap days for 2,000 years. It was an exceptional result for now there were the leap days for 1,000, 2,000, 3,000, 7,000 and 24,000 years and all in the same group of men from Bethlehem.

It was outlined earlier that because of the checksum totals, there was likely to be an error of between 3 to 6 extra units (days) in the overall totals. Interestingly, there appeared to be a provocative anomaly of 4 with the men from Bethlehem. Indeed, that anomaly was specifically highlighted because the two men Lod Hadid Ono and Jericho were reversed on the two lists. (A reversal of names brought to mind the crossover encountered earlier where Ephraim and Manasseh had switched positions in the two censuses of the tribes of Israel. In that case the number 36,500, with its notable equivalent of 100 solar years had been encountered beneath the computations. In this presentation, and adjacent to where the two men had also switched places, was the number 365 or the equivalent to one solar year. Two switches of names with two presentation of the solar year to bear witness.) If the number 4 was removed, the totals of the four anomalies in the men from Bethlehem would add up to a total of 677. That figure was the equivalent in whole days as the number of leap days for half the cycle of the Zodiac of 12,960 years. That anomaly, which was reflected in the two checksums, seemed to have been devised to draw attention to its side affects when subtracted from the totals of the men from Bethlehem. Therefore, it was deducted that the checksum anomaly with 3 extra units had been deliberately intended and should be utilised to probe further into the figures. This whole venture beyond the face value of mere numbers and associated comparable anomalies between the two sets of figures was intriguing. But sometimes it appeared to be intelligently designed. It was like playing a game of chess on a table with the scribes from the time of Ezra and Nehemiah sitting opposite having anticipated every move.

Allowing that this adjustment of minus 3 (days) could be applied, the numbers of the men from Bethlehem were again scrutinised. The two totals of 104 and 365 had been shown to match up with 2,000 and 7,000 years. That only left the number 212 and as leap days, it matched up with 4,061 years. By reducing that number of 212 by 3, the result of 209 matched up exactly with 4,000 years. A sequence was developing for the numbers of 1,000, 2,000, 3,000 had been outlined above and now it was followed by the number 4,000. The calculations continued with an adjustment of minus 3 being factored in as required and the complete findings were as follows:

- $212 + 104 - 3 = 313$, which was the equivalent number to the leap days for 6,000 years

- $104 + 365 = 469$, which was the equivalent number to the leap days for 9,000 years

- $212 + 365 - 3 = 574$, which was the equivalent number to the leap days for 11,000 years

- $212 + 104 + 365 - 3 = 676$, which was the equivalent number to the leap days for 12,960 years

Table 4: The Men from Bethlehem

Names	Ezra	Nehemiah	Ezra	Ezra +	Neh. +	Comments
Bethlehem	123	188			65	
Netophah	56		56			
Anathoth	128	128				
Azmaveth	42	42				
Kiriath J K and B	743	743				
Ramah and Geha	621	621				
Michmash	122	122				
Bethel and Ai	223	123		100		
Nebo	52	52				Leap days for 1,000 years
Magbish	156		156			Leap days for 3,000 years
other Elam	1,254	1,254				Leap days for 24,000 years
Harim	320	320				
Lod Hadid Ono	**725**	**721**		4		Reversed with Jericho
Jericho	**345**	**345**				reversed with Lod hadid Ono
Senaah	3,630	3,930			300	
Totals	**8,540**	**8,589**	**212**	**104**	**365**	**Total 17,810**

Those results had completed a grand sequence with 1,000, 2,000, 3,000, 4,000, 6,000, 9,000, 11,000 and 24,000 so it was safe to list them as years. In addition to those eight results, the period of 12,960 years was identifiable. In all, that was a total of nine periods which were the root and branch of the temple calendar. Because of the consistency in forming the periods in sequence it confirmed that applying the anomaly of minus 3 had been justified. That reference in Revelation to "Fallen! Fallen is Babylon" had acquired a new image for when that empire fell the men from Bethlehem came home. The findings practically mirrored the table derived from the periods and numbers in the Book of Revelation, which was influenced by Jesus. Appropriately, it was the men from Bethlehem who delivered the treasure chest of numbers.

THE FINAL CHECKSUM

In the earlier analysis, the period of a temple month had been outlined as 31.3194 days but for a workable model the period of 31 ¼ days was utilised. Jesus or the meticulous scribes were unlikely to leave such an important measurement to chance. Therefore, evidence was sought to see if they had utilised that more manageable figure of 31 ¼ days for the temple month. The difference between 31.3194 days and 31 ¼ days was 0.0694 of a day. The temple month was derived from the period of 600 years, which was the period that it matched up with. But what sort of an indicator could Jesus have left to demonstrate the workable model of the temple month? It seemed that the period when one correcting leap day had to be added would be the likely indicator. In the solar 365 day calendar it would have been every 14.4 years so that option was neither viable nor unique enough to be recognised as a milestone. The adjustment was to the temple month so perhaps the indicator was inserted within that calendar framework. Because the temple month derived from 600 years, that period would be the natural base to start from. It would take 14.4 times that number of 600 years before one whole leap day had accrued to be added in. That multiplied out to a lengthy period of 8,640 years. Ironically, that period of 8,640 years was the length of four constellations of the Zodiac where 2,160 × 4 = 8,640 years. The search resumed by looking in the Book of Revelation for evidence in some shape or format to decide the issue of temple month. Would it be like searching for the proverbial needle in a haystack? However, it turned out to be a relatively simple task to reveal the number of 8,640 for it presented itself when all the time periods quoted in Revelation were added up as follows:

Chapter 2	10 days
Chapter 9	5 months plus 5 months
Chapter 10	1 year, 1 month, 1 day and 1 hour
Chapter 11	42 months, 1,260 days, 3.5 days and 3.5 days
Chapter 12	1,260 days
Chapter 13	42 months
Chapter 17	1 hour
Chapter 18	1 day and also 1 hour cited 3 times
Chapter 20	1,000 years cited 6 times
Total	**8,640 or 2,160 × 4**

Note. It should be noted that there are eight and a half hours cited in Revelation but only four of them are specifically listed as "one hour." The remainder are cited as "an hour." There is one exception for in Chapter 10 there is no such ambiguity for the four period of a year, a month, a day and an hour clearly declare that 'an hour' in that context has the same status as the other three periods.

The total of all the periods when added up as just neutral numbers came to the numerical value of four constellations at 8,640 years. This outcome was achieved irrespective of the periods being hours, days, months and years. Not alone had the 8,640 been revealed, but it also was a prime example to show that the various time periods could be converted to just neutral numbers. It also was the evidence to indicate that the workable model of 31 ¼ leap days was used for the temple month. That result was perhaps the ultimate demonstration of a viable checksum and its value of 8,640 with its equivalent of four constellations had proven the time periods quoted in Revelation to have retained their original values intact.

The relevant numbers and time periods in the Book of Revelation had proven to be intelligently designed so as to measure time with the temple year of 777 days. It was a book that was influenced by Jesus who, as a carpenter, would have been well versed with numbers and measurements. Therefore, it was reasonable to suggest that we have witnessed the first fruits of his covert numerical skills.

CHAPTER 10

203

Church of Mary Magdelene, Jerusalem

CHAPTER 11

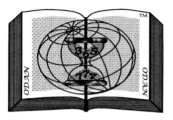

THE WORD ALONE WAS NOT ALMIGHTY

The language of science is maths and it is full of amazing theorems. Today's theories are tomorrow's facts and the evidence is real, being either visibly apparent or ridigidly tested until proved to be academically acceptable. But equally important is that the language of mathematics is universal, transcends time, space and cultural translation. In contrast, the language of biblical religions heretofore was in the ambiguous medium of words. A word can mean anything I want it to mean was set in stone by Lewis Carroll and that is surely the greatest dilemma for biblical enthusiasts. Their source of inspiration is the Bible, a book that is full of contradictions. A story written in any language is open to vast interpretation of the words therein, so consider the status of the Bible? It has been translated from ancient Hebrew and Greek into English and every other common language in use today. The one major saviour for the authenticity of the original text of the good book was that a two thousand year old version of the Book of Isaiah was found among the Dead Sea Scrolls. That version compared almost exactly to the Biblical version, which was handed down from generation to generation. But even with that redemption, the credibility of the words and claims of the Bible are largely undermined by exaggerated tales that could never be more than bedtime nursery stories.

How different the Bible has proved to be in these research findings where it was outlined in the medium of numbers and mathematical proofs. Those results excelled because arithmetic is a language that is pure, universal and one could argue that it is even infallible. Heretofore, the god of the ancient Hebrews appeared to have been mathematically illiterate and had not provided the numerical evidence to support the divine advertisement stating that *God made the world*. To the rationally minded person, religious beliefs thrived on ignorance and superstition in a vacuumed culture where priestly males dominated and education was denied to the masses or imposed with censored rigour. From these findings there can be no doubt that the Israelites possessed a knowledge which originated from a superior source. But where did such an advanced knowledge of the heavens originate from? Was there once a higher intelligence, be it a successive league of Einstein's, or some divine like force that is alien to our limited mediational abilities? If such a diverse media did address our ancestors, then they obviously spoke in a higher language that has long been lost in history?

In such an amnesia void, the dominant successors could only rule by trying to maintain the status quo and ban the elements that they themselves did not understand. Within that vacuum, the right to rule was regally promoted as divinely inspired and the carriers viewed such fundamental rights as obligatory for the masses to obey the god given commands. It was the glory days of Pharaohs and Caesars. Kings, Queens, Tsars and Kaisers thrived on that doctrine and paraded in wealth adorned by robes and rituals. The 20th century flushed out those later tyrannies. It was a new dawn for enlightenment. But, lost forever in the bonfires were vast libraries and scrolls from the ancients. Unbelievably, the Bible survived and so did the Dead Sea Scrolls. But the ability to understand their enigmatic language was not passed on. A language so ambiguous with its cryptic 'crossword' jargon that was so eminent with the prophets and scribes? The faithful therefore stuck to the easier path of blind faith with its stepping-stones of words, rather than tread the higher-minded depths of profound logic.

Birth place of the Virgin Mary

CHAPTER 12

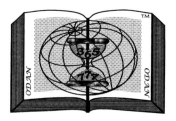

THE WOMEN WHO ENDURED

The women that were profiled in the Messiah blood line were exposed to many strange encounters some of which had sexual overtones that were very much out of character with the austere theme of biblical purity. The first encounter was with Sarah and Abraham. To protect himself, Abraham had pretended that his wife Sarah was his sister when he went to Egypt. Because of her beauty, word reached Pharaoh and she was brought to his palace and they ended up in bed together. In case it would be seen that Abraham made an innocent mistake the scribes included a second version. That was where Abraham again passed of Sarah as his sister to King Abimelech who took her. Strangely perhaps, in both instances when the deception was discovered, Abraham was rewarded with valuables and livestock. It appeared that Abraham's son Isaac learned nothing from his father's actions for he too compromised his wife Rebecca when he passed her off as his sister to that same king. The king observed the couple behaving intimately in the palace gardens and latched onto the deception. Jacob and Rachel went through the marriage ceremony festivities, but her sister Leah was sent into the bridal suite and slept with him on that wedding night. Three women and the roles of sisters was a common factor and all involved deception. Rebecca had twins and biblical sources state that Leah and Rachel were twins. Judah reneged on his widowed daughter in law Tamar but fathered twins by her in an act of prostitution at a wayside tent. When Tamar was given birth, the mid-wife tied a red thread around the wrist of one of the boys.

That red thread would lead the way to the next high pro-filed woman in the Messiah time line. Rehab was the harlot that helped the spies escape from Jericho before it was attacked by the Israelites. Being strangers in Jericho, the spies had obviously selected the open door abode of a harlot to find shelter. But the story of Rehab had an almighty twist. Those were not the first spies to be sent into the Promised Land for Moses had previously sent out twelve men. When those spies had come back they outlined that the walls of the cities before them reached up to the heavens. Ten of those men were slain by the Lord but two were saved. Now two spies were in the house of Rehab, which was on top of the city wall. The local security forces came looking for the spies but Rehab sent the two men up onto the roof and hid them beneath bales of flax. After sending the searching guards on a wild goose chase she made a pact with the two men who agreed to ensure that her family would be saved in the oncoming attack because she had saved them. She then helped the two men escape from on high out through her window by a chord all the way down the city wall. They asked her to tie a scarlet thread on the escape window so that the attackers could know to avoid her house and thus prevent any blood being spilt with her family.

Rehab and her family were in the house that was on top of the walls of Jericho. And previously the spies had told Moses that the city walls in the Promised Land reached up into the heavens. Rehab and her family were all saved in the ensuing onslaught so the red thread obviously worked. But how could they be saved for as most people know, the walls of Jericho fell down flat when the seven priests blew on seven trumpets after circling the city seven times. And Rehab's house was on top of those very walls. So there was a deeper dimension to the story outline and it would appear that Rehab was somehow suspended in mid-air looking down at the flattened walls beneath. Was that chord on which the spies escaped akin to Jacob's ladder that reached the heavens? If so, the Promised Land appeared to have had that alternative dimension and the scarlet thread was the link to the Messiah time line. The cluster of sevens was there to support that view that the heavens was the real objective and the outcome of the events brought the Messiah time line into view. In that encounter at Jericho, be it with the two spies or a subsequent relationship, Rehab became pregnant for she was named as one of the women in the Messiah blood line. Indeed, she was the mother of the first son in both genealogies to be born in the Promised Land. The red thread with Tamar and a scarlet thread with Rehab, and both had saved the genealogies of the Messiah time line. The story also revealed that being a harlot was not an obstacle to reaching the pinnacle of the heavens or becoming the matriarch of the Messiah.

Ruth was the next woman to save the Messiah genealogy and appropriately enough, it was at Bethlehem. She was a Moabite, the widowed daughter-in-law of Naomi whom she accompanied on her return to her homeland. It was outlined above how she had slept at the feet of the elder Boaz on the threshing floor. Boaz had treated Ruth as an equal and had warned all the young men to treat her well. After the encounter on the threshing floor, Boaz went through a consultative process with the elders and established that a Moabite alien like Ruth could become the rightful inheritor of his estate. They got married and Ruth became the mother of Obed and the grandmother of Jesse. A rod out of the stem of Jesse would become king over all Israel. The link back to Tamar was firmly established for the short genealogy in the Book of Ruth began with Perez the son of Tamar and traced the lineage to Boaz, Obed, Jesse and David. So Ruth became the great grandmother of David.

The Final Residence of the Virgin Mary

The story moved on to when David was king and where he was provoked to the point of killing a man called Nabal. However, Nabal's wife Abigail brought gifts to David and gave him sound advice. Nabal died soon after in a drunken stupor and David married the widowed Abigail. In due course Abigail became the mother of Nathan. Time went by and one day David wandered from his bed onto the palace roof from where he saw a woman washing herself. He greatly admired her beauty. Her name was Bathsheba and she was the wife of Uriah. David sent messengers to bring Bathsheba to his palace and he made love to her. She became pregnant and David's desires for her must have been insatiable for he contrived to have her husband killed. He arranged that Uriah should be sent to the front line in battle where life was cheap. Uriah was killed so David married the beautiful widowed Bathsheba. But the Lord was angry and the child died. Bathsheba conceived again and became the mother of Solomon.

Bathsheba is considered to have been an adulteress by biblical commentators but men would take that shallow view. Did she have any choice in the matter seeing that David was the king? That suggestion that she was compromised arose from the similarity of the story in the very next chapter in Samuel2 where David's son Amnon believed he was in love with his step sister Tamar. (Another Tamar) Amnon pretended to be ill and asked his father David to send Tamar to him so that he could eat from her hand. When Tamar entered his bedroom he grabbed her and said *come to bed with me my sister.* She pleaded with him saying *don't force me for such an act should not be done in Israel.* He raped her but King David on hearing of it did nothing. So it was left to Tamar's brother Absalom to kill Amnon for disgracing his sister. Therefore, it would appear that David had condoned his son Amnon raping his daughter Tamar and by implication, he appeared to have treated Bathsheba in like fashion. The Lord made David see the error of his ways through a story about sheep and a ewe lamb and the king relented. The linkage with sheep was evident for previously Judah had gone sheep sheering when he encountered Tamar. Abraham had compromised Sarah to King Abimelech and later he made a treaty with him and gave him seven ewe lambs. Rachel was watering her sheep when she met Jacob and she was compromised by having to stand back while her sister Leah was sent into the bridal suite. Finally, shepherds would come to visit the infant Jesus, thus again highlighting the importance of sheep into the Messianic time line.

The way was thus prepared for the next in line, Mary, who was destined to become pregnant from on high with the most important infant in the Bible. She was to be married to Joseph but he noticed she was pregnant. He wanted to protect her and so they got married. Later on at the time of a census, they went up to Bethlehem to be counted but there was no room at the Inn when her son was born. Nearby shepherds who were minding their sheep came to pay homage to the baby Jesus. Like Jacob, Mary too would oscillate between two split personalities. One personality was the pure fourteen year old virgin who was accosted by an angel. The other profile is a subject of controversial association between Mary the mother of Jesus and Mary Magdalene, his favourite companion. Under Jewish austere laws the first Mary should have been stoned for getting pregnant outside marriage even though she was just fourteen years old. That man made law was conveyed in the most public terms when the other Mary came running from the mob and found herself at the feet of Jesus. The writing was on the wall with Daniel but with Jesus it was in the sand at the very feet of Mary Magdalene. What did he write in the sands of time? Was it Sarah, Hagar, Rebecca, Leah, Rachel, Tamar, Rehab, Deborah, Ruth, Hannah, Abigail, Bathsheba, Esther, Judith, Elizabeth and Mary? Those were the names of the prominent women who featured in the Messiah time line.

Hollow Church, Laois

Conclusion

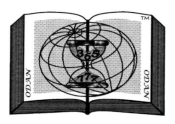

It is not practical to write a conclusion yet because the research work is still progressing. However, there are enough discoveries in this book to boost the image of the Bible and show it to be the greatest wonder of the ancient world. It is all so mysterious and fundamental questions abound. The magnitude and impact are so vast that the three principle religions of Judaism, Christianity and Islam will have some considerable issues to address. For thousands of years, rabbis, priests, clerics and scholars have interpreted the Bible and the faiths of millions rested on the written word. But the one true universal language has proved to be numbers and the medium to mediate with God was the ether of time.

Michael

On Killiney Hill

EPILOGUE

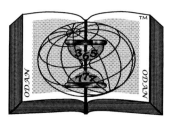

In the 1st century AD, the Jewish historian Josephus raised a very unusual subject concerning the ancient Hebrews. He stated that the descendants of Adam possessed a great wisdom of the heavenly bodies. Aware of the pending deluge the ancients wrote this knowledge on two pillars so as to preserve it for future generations. In the Book of Enoch it stated that the children of the heavens took wives on earth and to them were born giants. The story in Enoch related that those heavenly beings brought evil upon the earth and taught men astrology, the constellations, the signs of the earth, sun and the course of the moon. In fact it stated that they revealed the eternal secrets which were preserved in heaven. Their behaviour was so outrageous to the lord above that he intervened with the flood and destroyed mankind with the deluge. That reference to a great wisdom was also reflected in the theme with the Garden of Eden except in that scene, it was the tree of life and the tree of knowledge that were the two pillars of wisdom.

Josephus also made a specific reference to the generations relative to the unbelievable ages of Adam and Noah's descendant where he stated:

"God afforded them a longer time of life on account of their virtue and the good use they made of it in astronomical and geometrical discoveries, which would not have afforded the time of foretelling (the periods of the stars) unless they had lived 600 years; for the great year is completed in that interval." Josephus 1.3.9

Nobody in their right mind would accept those incredible figures of Adam's generations living to nigh on 900 years and some of Noah's descendants surviving to between 119 to 500 years. Perhaps it could be argued that a year in that bygone era was not the 365 days that we know.

Taking the expression of increase and multiply as a hint the numbers in those two lists of incredible ages were multiplied together. Just as with the computations with the two censuses, the results led the research into a mind maze that had recognisable measurements of the heavens. From such a simple instruction the door into the beyond was finally opened to reveal an incredible matrix of time that lay behind the computations. The long lost wisdom of the ancients had at last been found.

To be published in 2009 by JD McKenzie

Notes

Note 1 Reference the book "Number" McLeish John,
Published by Bloomsbury, London WlV 5DE 1991

Note 2 The solar year is 365.242199 days long though for
calendar purposes 365.25 days are used so as to add a leap
day every four years. Because of that position there are some
longer term corrections involving further leap days. The orbits of the planets are Venus = 224.7 days, Mars = 687 days,
Jupiter = 4,332.59 days, Saturn = 10,759.2 days. The lunar
orbit is 29.53 days or 354.35 days in a Lunar year.

Note 3 There were fundamental problems with this theory of
counting out the days for it is believed that most ancient
civilisations only knew how to count in a series of ones. In
those primitive times the abacus was the calculator for it just
required moving one bead every day to count the days. That
was the simplest form of counting for it did not include our
automatically accepted positional system of addition when
counting above the single digit of nine. Modern mathematics
employs this base ten system of arithmetic with the inbuilt
zero and fractions of up to one, two and three places of
decimal etc. The ancients were not reckoned to have been so
mathematically sophisticated and even the Greeks did not
have the invisible zero. It is believed that the ancient Sumer-
ians had a zero in their maths while the Egyptians did count
in tens and had developed a system of fractions. The Babylonians employed base-sixty mathematics, which is very evident
in the 24 hour clock I.e. 60 seconds, 60 minutes.

Note 4 Chapters 28, 29 Books of Numbers, Chronicles1 29:21,
Chronicles2 29:21:32, Ezra 6:17, 8:35

Note 5 Ref. "Who Wrote the Bible" by Richard Elliot Friedman,
Harper Publisher 1997

Note 6 The scribes had referred many times to their army formations in such groupings as captains over hundreds, thousands etc. so the principal of counting in that manner was well established.

Note 7 It was found in Ezekiel 40:3:6, Zechariah 2:1 Amos 7:7-9 and Revelation 21:15.

Note 8 The most practical way to explain the importance of checksums is to outline how they are used to guarantee that the data transmitted from computers over the world networks arrive in the original format that they were sent. To do this the packets of data being transmitted are counted and the total as a number is inserted in the leading pre-packet. So when that total number of say 100 is received in the leading header packet the incoming end knows to expect 100 packets of data. If 100 packets are received the data is valid but anything outside of 100 packets would entail all the data packets being rejected as invalid.

Note 9 Ref. Espenak Fred. NASA/Goddard Space Flight Centre, USA

Note 10 Ref. Encyclopaedia Britannica. P 419

Note 11 Those instructions are in the Book of Numbers Ch. 26:2:4:53:55:56.

Note 12 The Book of Numbers 32:33

Note 13 Because the fractions had been utilised as a plus factor of + 3 ½ days and a minus factor of – 1 ⅔ days it could be construed that undue liberty was been taken with adopting a minus element for one of the findings. The question was how would the scribes have conveyed to future generations that a minus computation had to be carried out? In addressing that dilemma the totals of all the numbers, optimal numbers and articles meaning '1' etc were counted up in Chapter 29 of Numbers and the result was 367. The total of the fractions added up to 1 ⅔. (Those were the fractions of 1 ⅔ that had been utilised as a minus value in the previous computations) It appeared that the wily scribes had deployed a very unique tempting way to convey that negative value for 367 and 1 ⅔ would trigger an automatic response to subtract the fractions and end up with the number of the solar year. i.e. 367 − 1 ⅔ = 365 ⅓ That type of arrangement was certainly unusual but yet there were similar examples in the overall findings to suggest that it was deliberately utilised as part of the verification process. Again, the solar year was the overall checksum.

Note 14 Much later in the research it was discovered that the ancient Greeks utilised that type of system of apportioning a common age to each generation as a calendar system.

Note 15 The Book of Jeremiah 25: 11:12 and Daniel 9: 20-27.

Note 16 Digging wells Genesis Ch. 22 and 26

Note 17 3,000 slain Exodus Ch. 32 :28. 250 consumed Numbers Ch. 16 : 35, Ch. 26 : 10 14,700 die of plague Numbers Ch.16 : 49. 24,000 die of plague Numbers Ch.25:9

Note 18 Leviticus 23:15-22

Note 19 Ref. John Mosley, Griffith Observatory, LA, California.

Note 20 The earlier finding with the 1,000 years from Solomon to Jesus at thirty years of age was anchored in Julian time relative to the Roman Emperor Tiberius being in his 15th year in office. He came to power in the year 14 CE which meant that it was in the year 28 or 29 CE when he was in his 15th year. That meant that Jesus would have been 34 or 35 in 29 CE relative to his birth in 5 or 4 BCE. So the Julian anchor of 29 AD was at odds with the heavenly orbital Saturn/Jupiter anchor of 5 or 4 BCE by four years. But there could be a natural explanation for the discrepancy. Before Tiberius came to power he was co-regent from 11 CE. If Luke had included that factor it would have meant that it was in the year 25 or 26 CE when the thirty year old Jesus began to preach.

Note 21 Exodus 37:10 for dimension of table and 2Chronicles Ch. 3 for dimensions of Solomon's Temple

Note 22 The Gospel of John 8:39

Note 23 For an alternative understanding of the events surrounding the death and resurrection of Jesus, reference "The Jesus Mystery" by Lena Einhorn, Publishers Robert Hale, London 2007. Also reference "How Jesus became Christian" by Barrie Wilson, Publishers Weidenfield & Nicolson, London 2008.

Note 24 The main reference Bible that was used throughout the research was the original KJV though for comparative purposes the Hebrew, Septuagint, Gideon and other Bibles were referenced, together with the Books of Enoch, Jasher, Jubilees and the lost gospels.

Bibliography

Barclay William

The Revelation of St John, Volume 2, Published by St Andrews Press Edinburgh 1959

Chilton Bruce

Redeeming Time, Publisher Hendrickson 2002, PO Box 3473, Peabody, Massachusetts

Duncan, David Ewing.

The Calendar, Published by Fourth Estate, London 1999.

Einhorn, Lena.

The Jesus Mystery , Published by Robert Hale, London 2007.

Espenak Fred

NASA/Goddard Space Flight Centre, USA.

Friedman Richard Elliot

Who Wrote the Bible, Harper Publishers 1997

Josephus

The Works of Josephus,. Published by Hendrickson MA 01961-3473 USA 2001

Kaplan Robert

The Nothing That Is (A Natural History of Zero), Published by Penguin Press, London 1999

Maxwell Marcus

Revelation, Published by the Bible Reading Fellowship, Oxford

McLeish John

Number,
Published by Bloomsbury, London
WIV 5DE 1991

North John

Astronomy and Cosmology,
Published by Fontana Press 1991

Stewart Ian

Nature's Numbers,
Published by Phoenix,
London 1995

Struik Dirk J

A Concise History of Mathematics,
Dover Publications, New York1987

The Bible.

King James, Revised English, Gideon, Septuagint. Books of Enoch,
Jubilees and Jasher

VanderKam James C.

Calendars in the Dead Sea scrolls,
Publishers Rutledge,
London NY 1998

Whitrow GJ

What is Time?
Publisher Thomas and Hudson,
London 1972

Wilson Barrie

How Jesus Became Christian,
Published by Weidenfield & Nicolson, London 2008

INDEX

DISCLAIMER

While every care has been taken in the compilation of this book, neither the author nor the publisher can accept responsibility for errors or omissions. Where such errors or omissions occur and are brought to our attention, they will be corrected for future editions of this book.

DISCLAIMER